Toby Mitchell

The Weekender

Copenhagen

COLLECTIVE SHORTS
by NHP PUBLISHING

As our plane made its final right turn to line up with runway 4R, I clocked that it was my tenth visit to the Danish capital. As I reminisced over the past nine visits, I began to think about why I've come back so many times. Of course there have been occasions for photoshoots, but the majority of trips were for time off and pure leisure.

For me, Copenhagen is a place that encapsulates inspiration and rest. Aside from my own country's capital, London, I've never visited another city more than Copenhagen.

Copenhagen holds some of the world's most innovative and creative minds as well as being globally esteemed for its pioneering legacy in design. Understatement, functionality and beauty are all words that not only articulate the aesthetic of the city itself but also the exports of creativity that come from its inhabitants.

As a photographer, I found it a significant creative challenge embarking on the task of trying to portray all that the city can be; from the work hard, rest hard culture, to the expansive array of outstanding independent food and drink offerings, to the un-deniably unique architecture...there is so much to bring justice to. I think even with my best efforts, I wouldn't be able to bring this European gold mine the honour it is due.

To really understand Copenhagen, you have to visit. When you walk the streets and observe how the locals live you will begin to understand that the lifestyle they pursue is nourishing to the mind, body and soul. Enjoying the outdoors, family life, friendship, good food and working hard from rest are all traits that I admire greatly about the lifestyle of the people of Copenhagen.

I partitioned this book into four sections; Thursday, Friday, Saturday and Sunday. The concept being as if *you* yourself are spending a long weekend in Copenhagen. This isn't a typical guide book as there are not specific recommendations on every page. However, there are a few suggestions that I have made as a direct result of my experiences when I visited. I hope that the following pages permeate the essence of Copenhagen and inspire you to visit one day soon. This city is so special to me and one of my absolute favourites. I hope that it becomes one of yours too.

Toby Mitchell

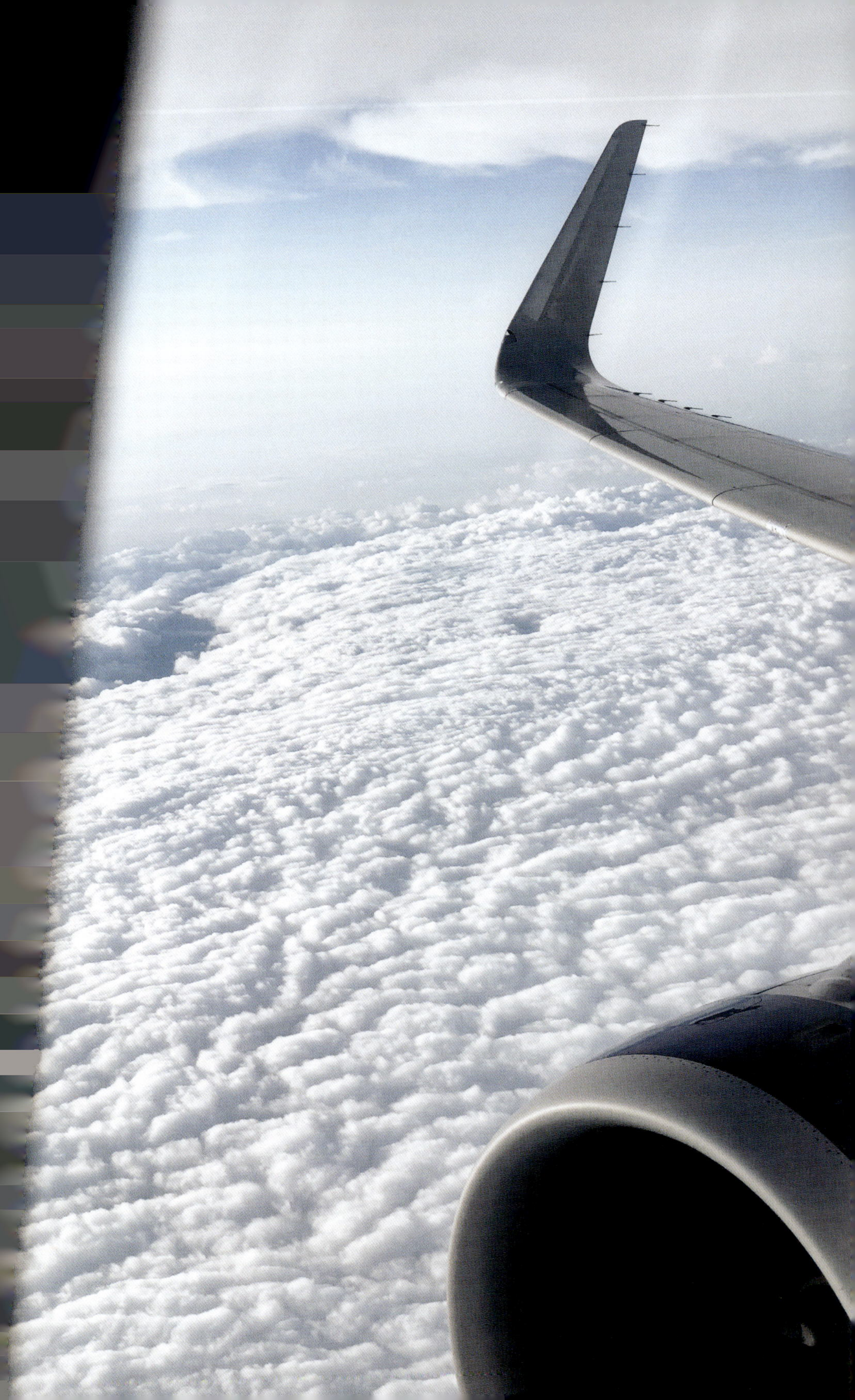

Thursday

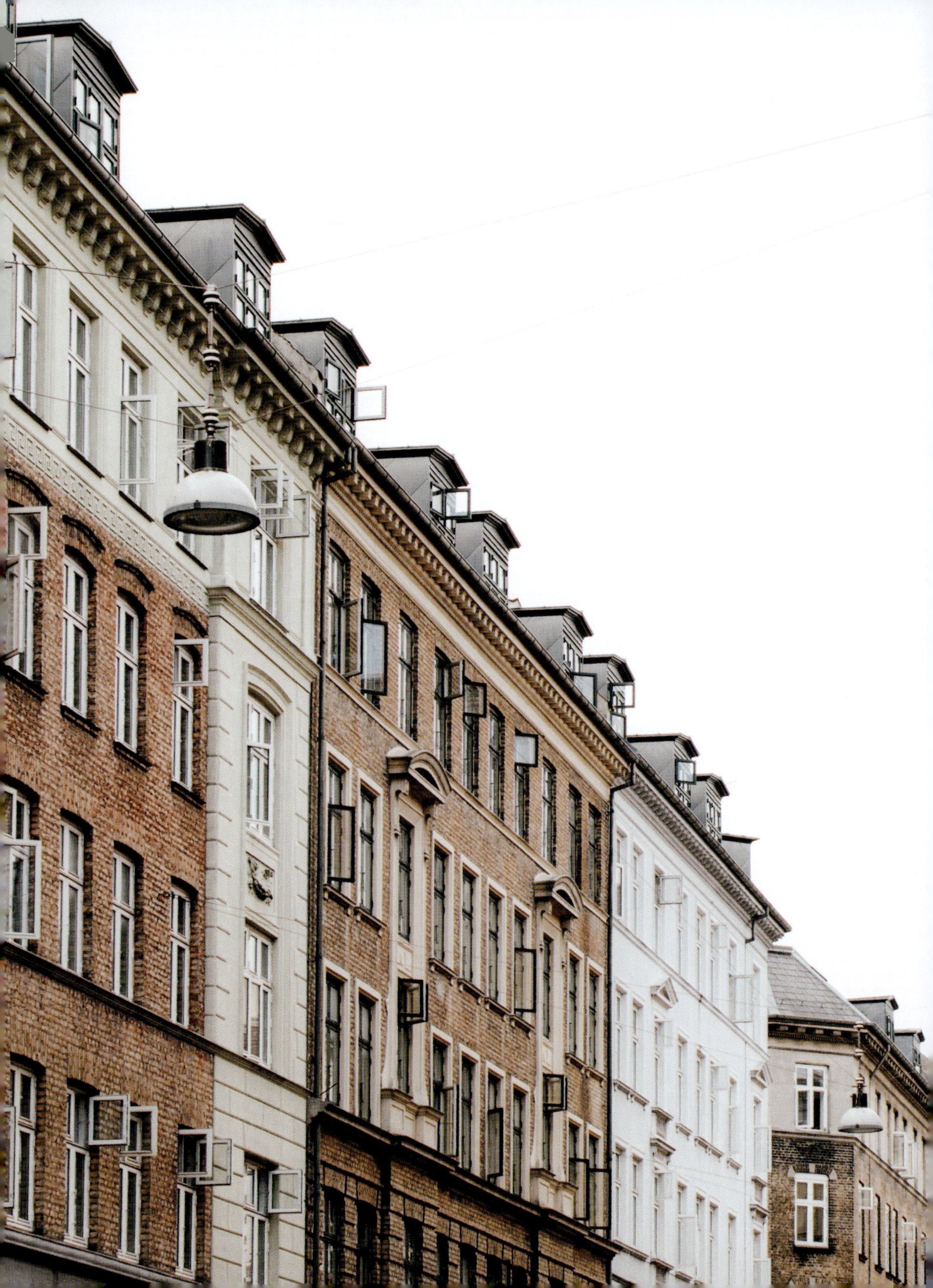

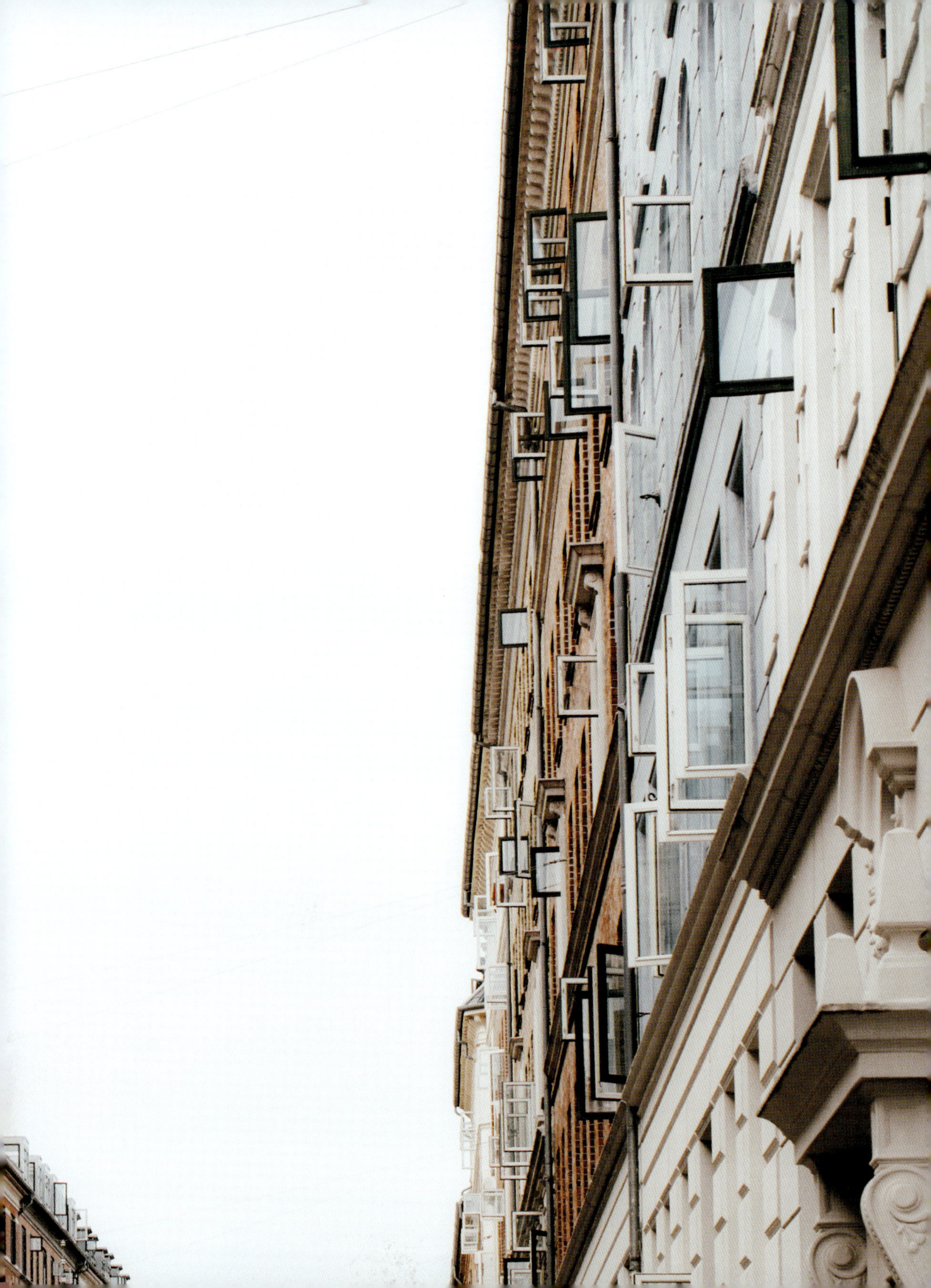

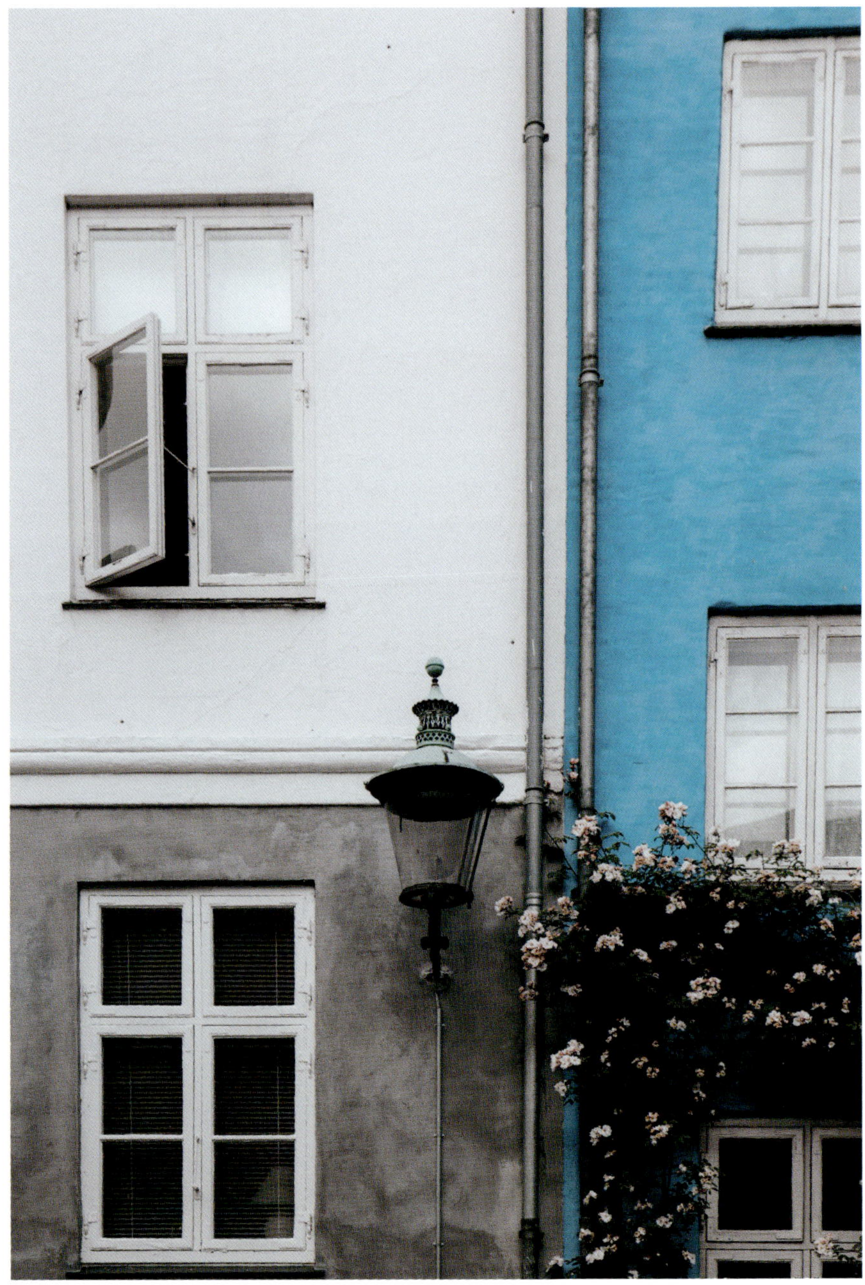

From the station to hotel

Thursday 2:35 PM

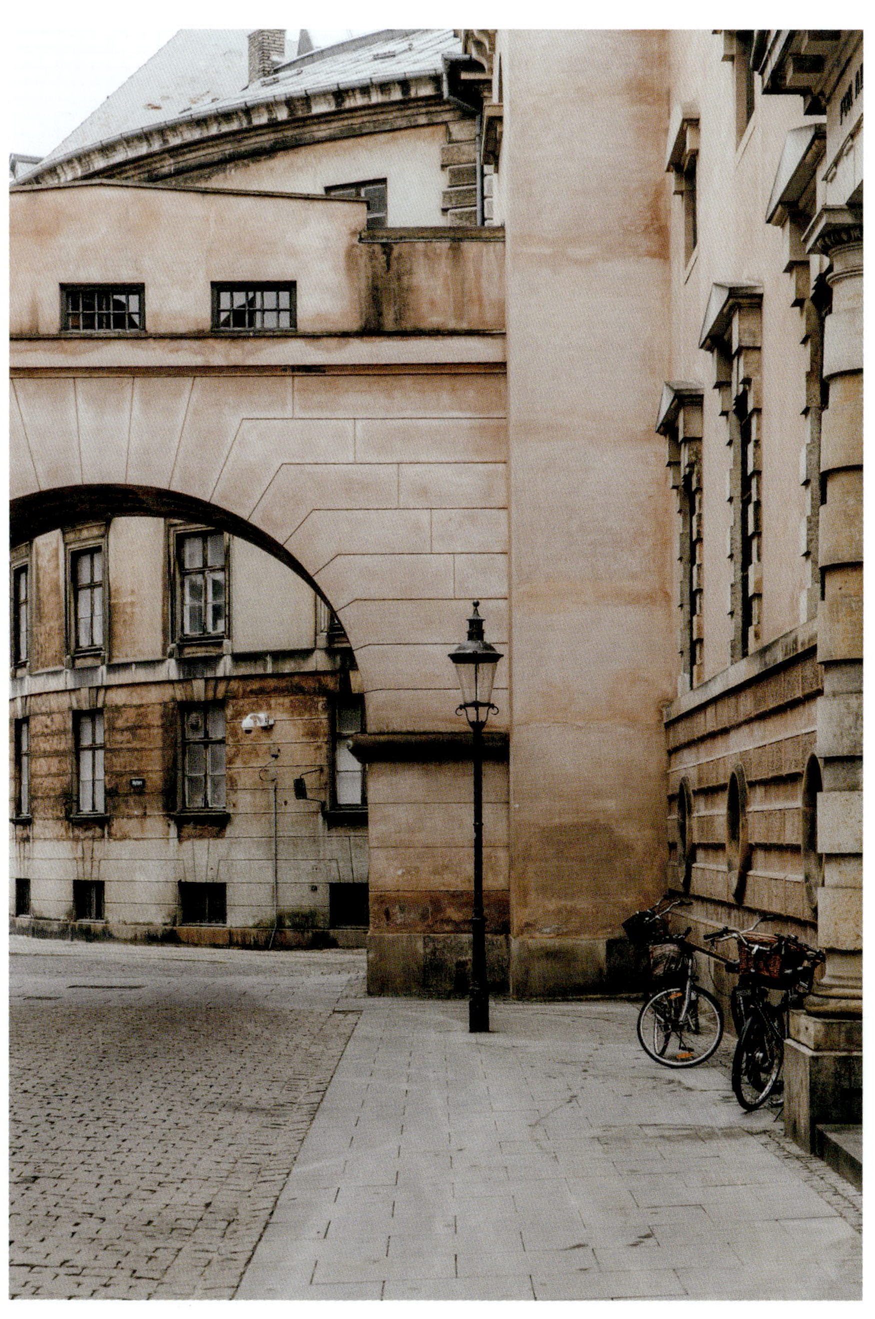

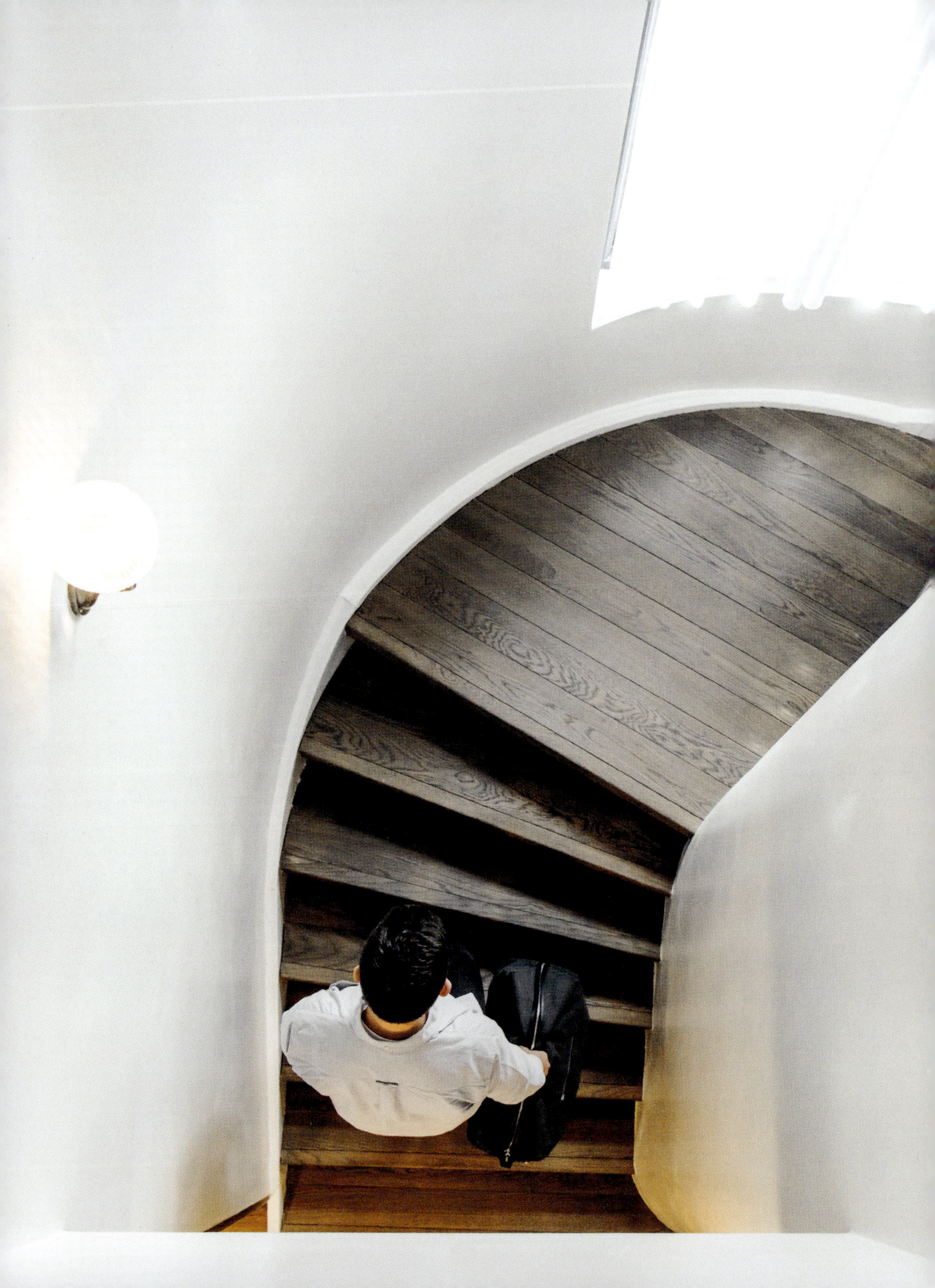

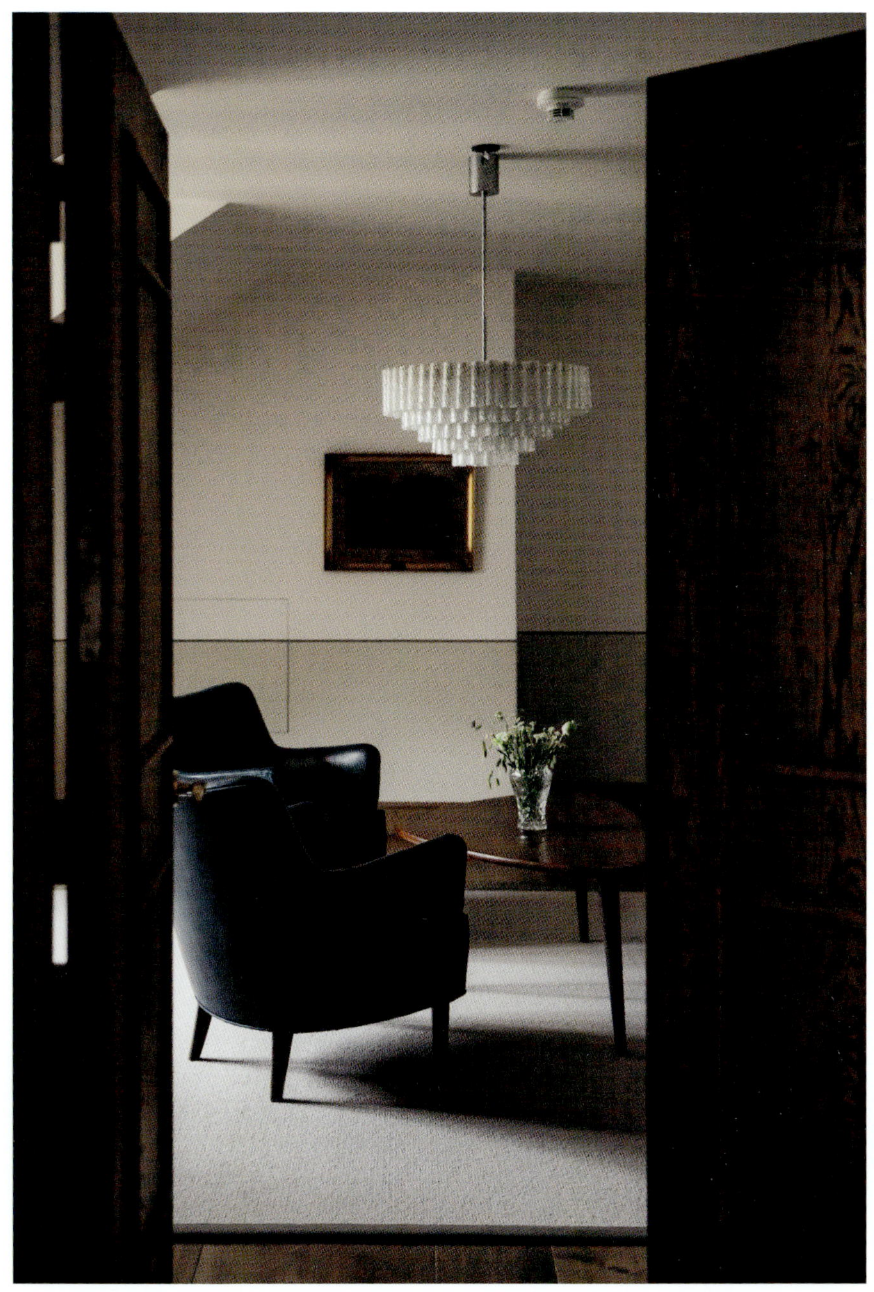

Thursday 3:00 PM

Arrival at Hotel Sanders

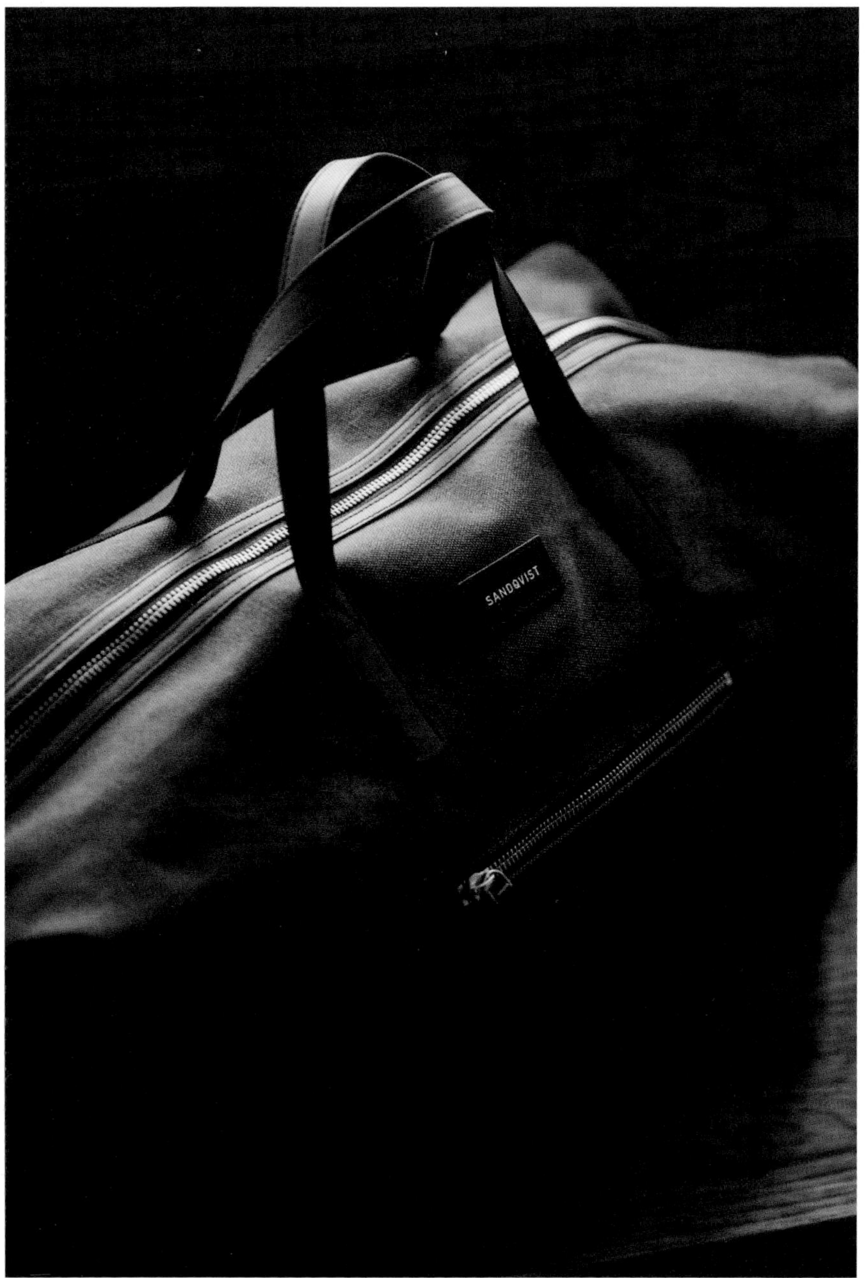
SANDQVIST

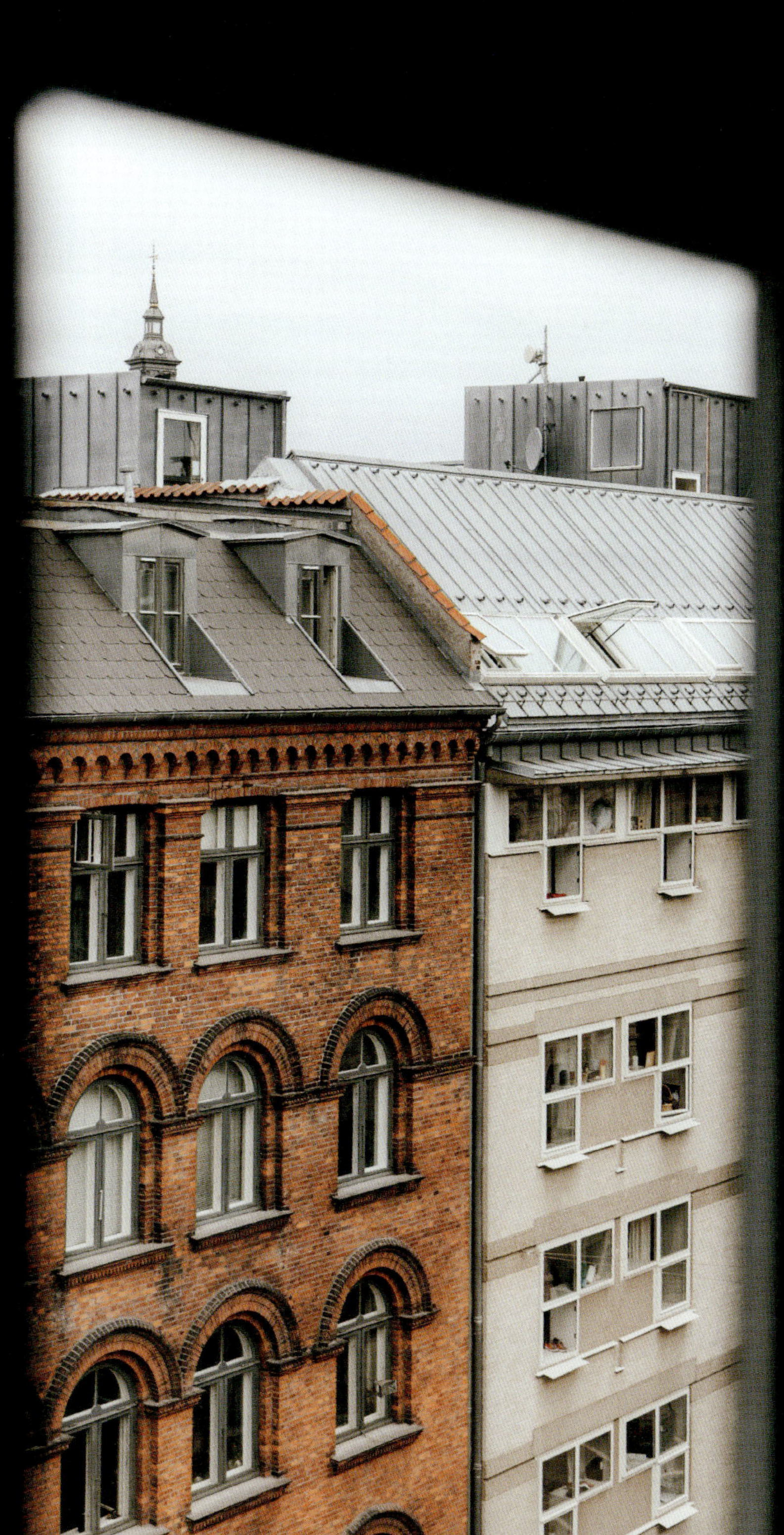

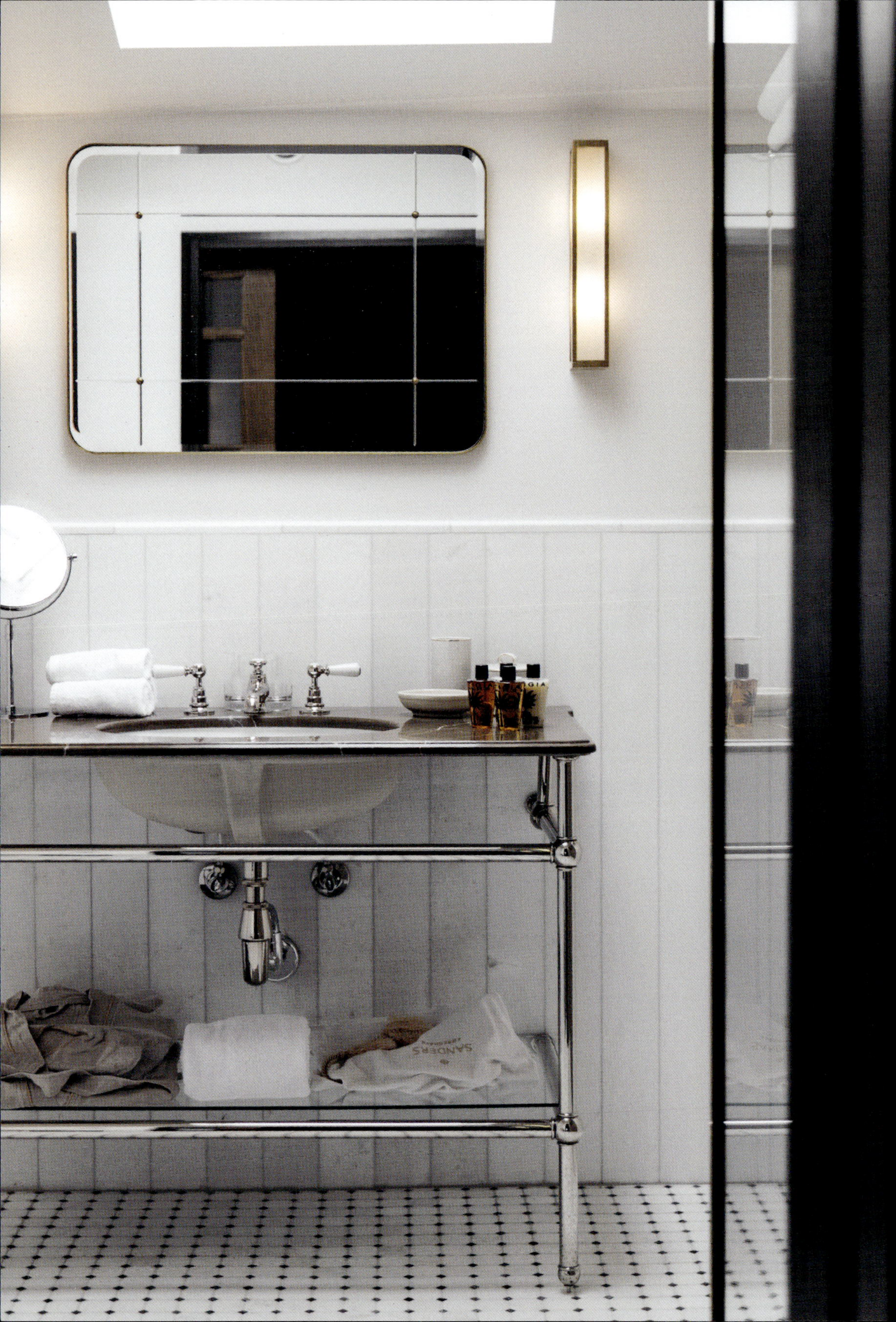
SANDERS

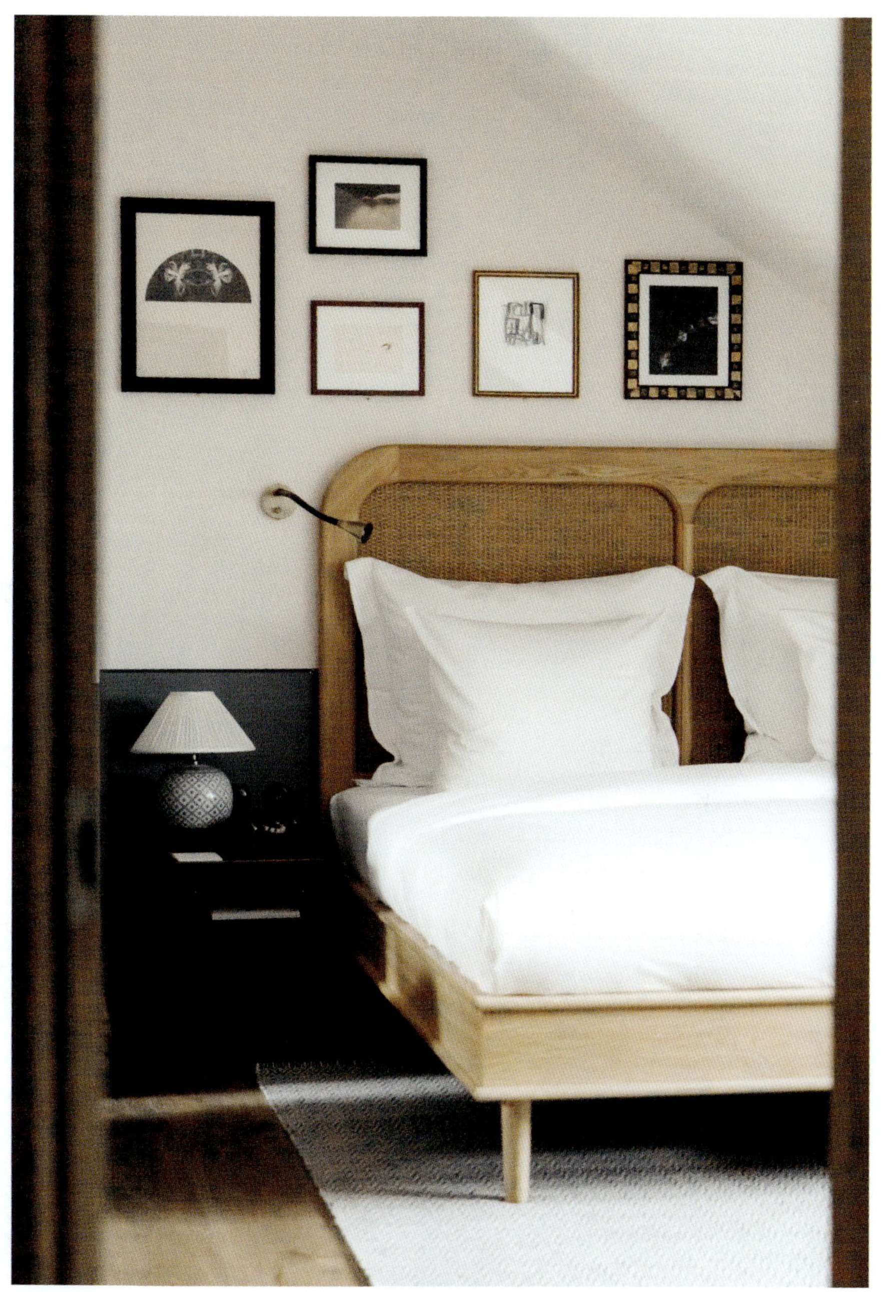

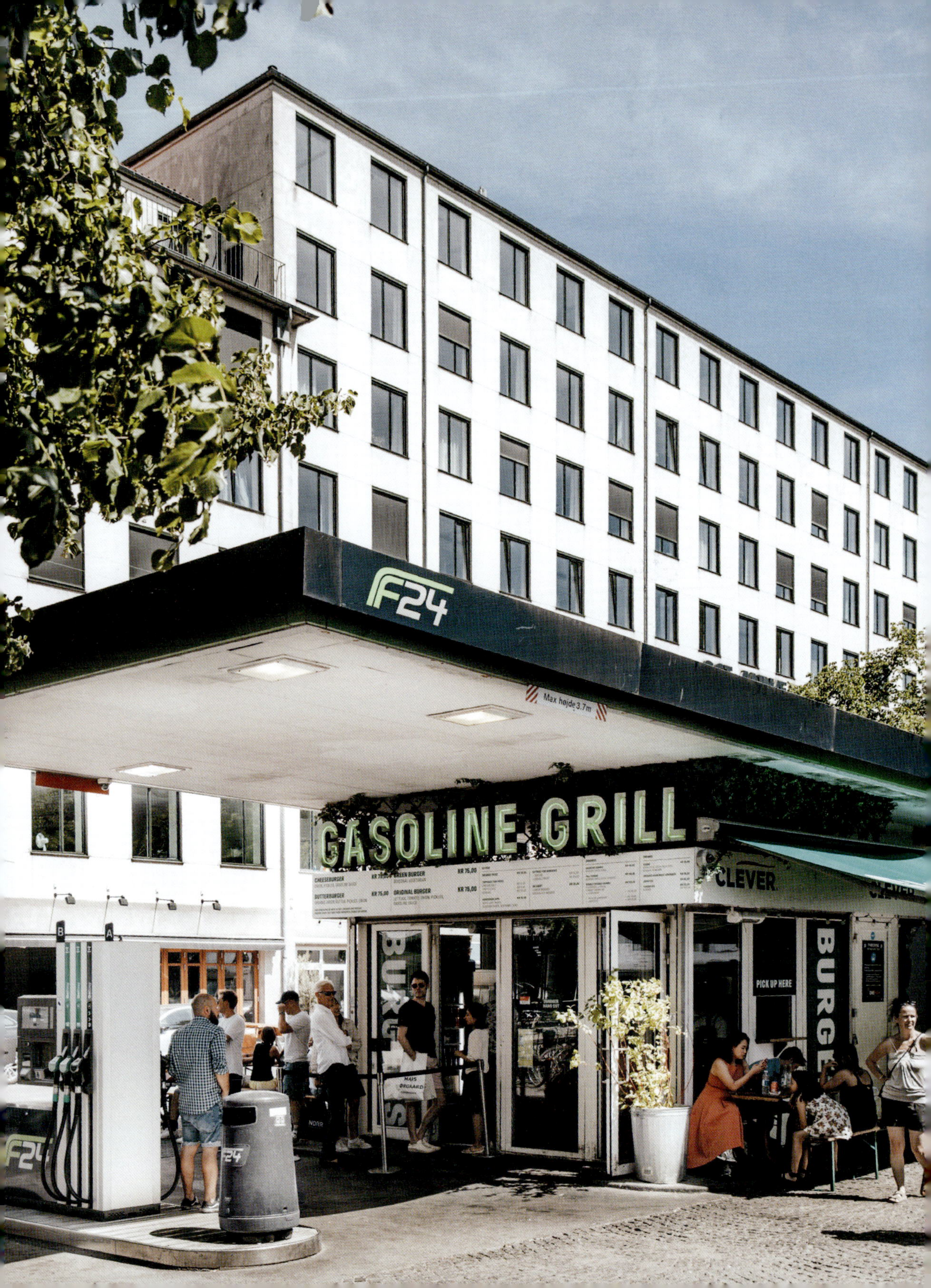

F24
Max højde 3,7m
GASOLINE GRILL
CLEVER
PICK UP HERE

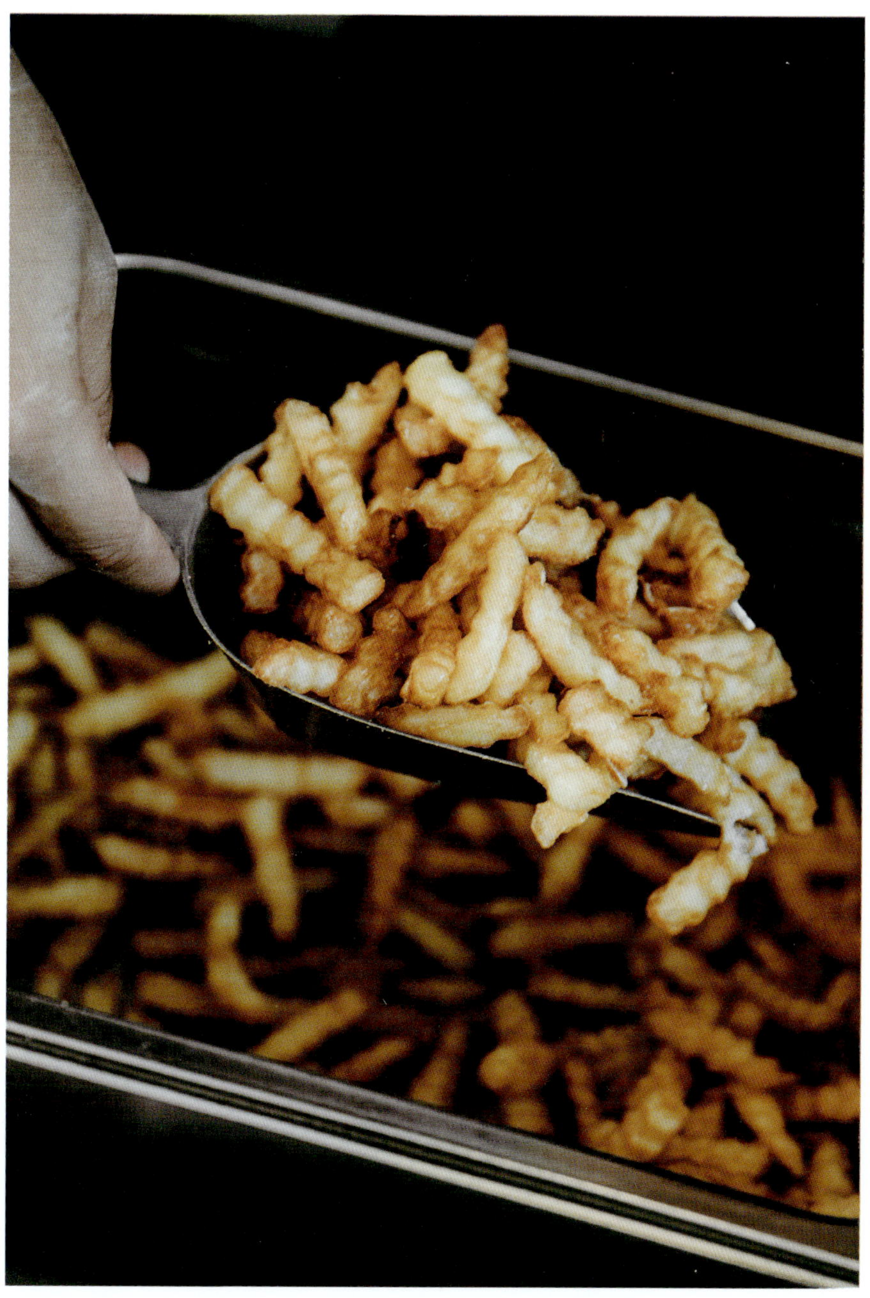

Thursday 5:16 PM

An early dinner

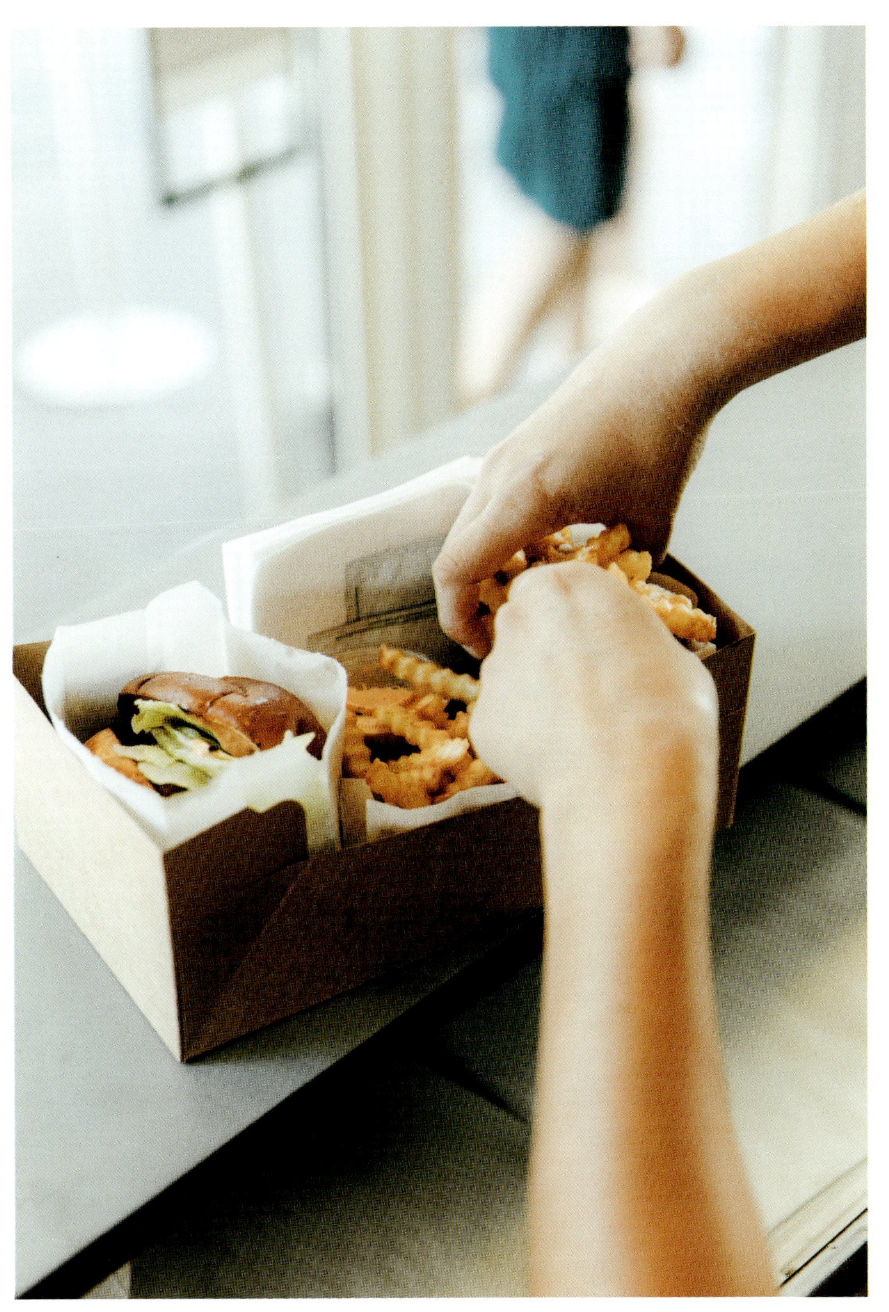

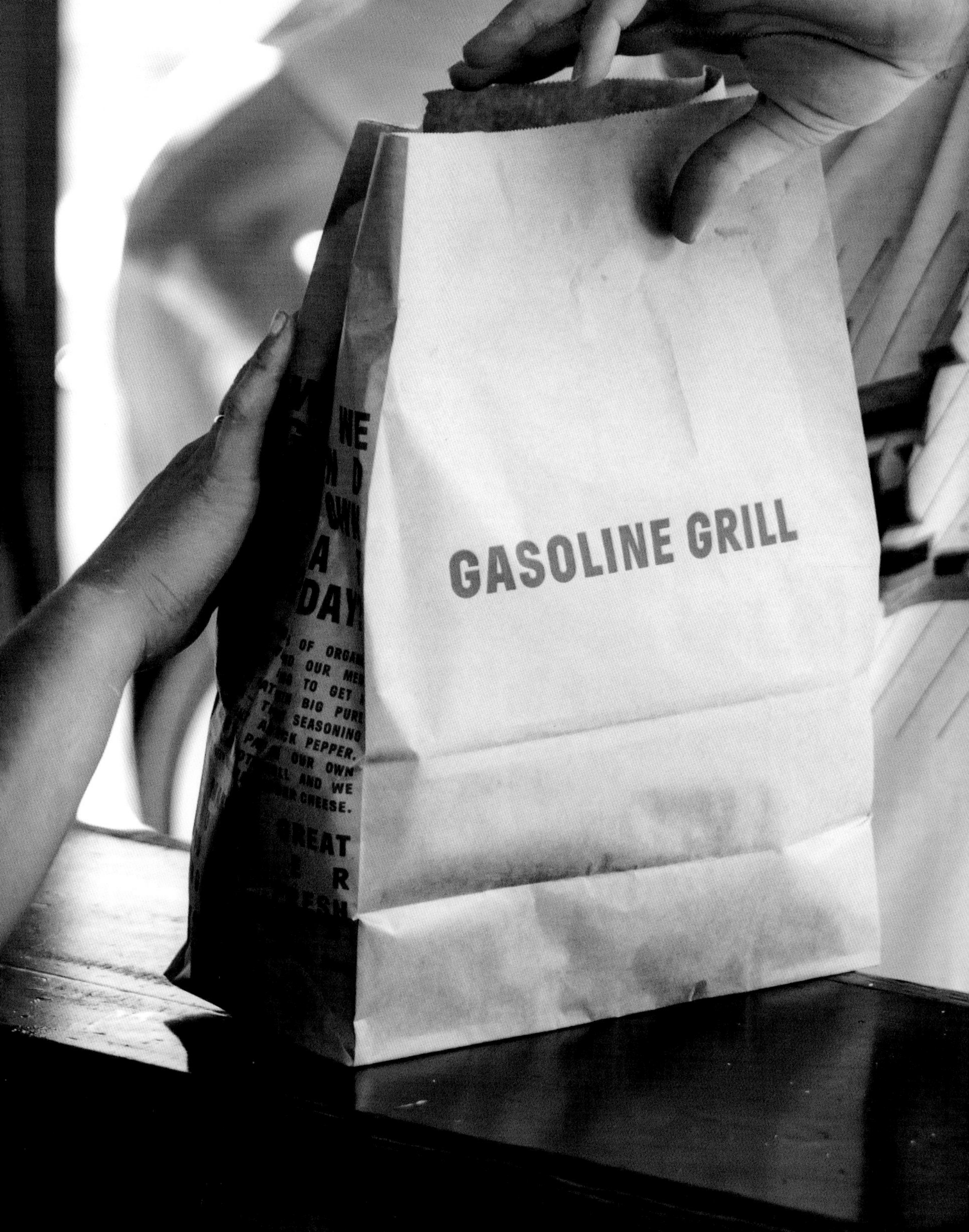
GASOLINE GRILL

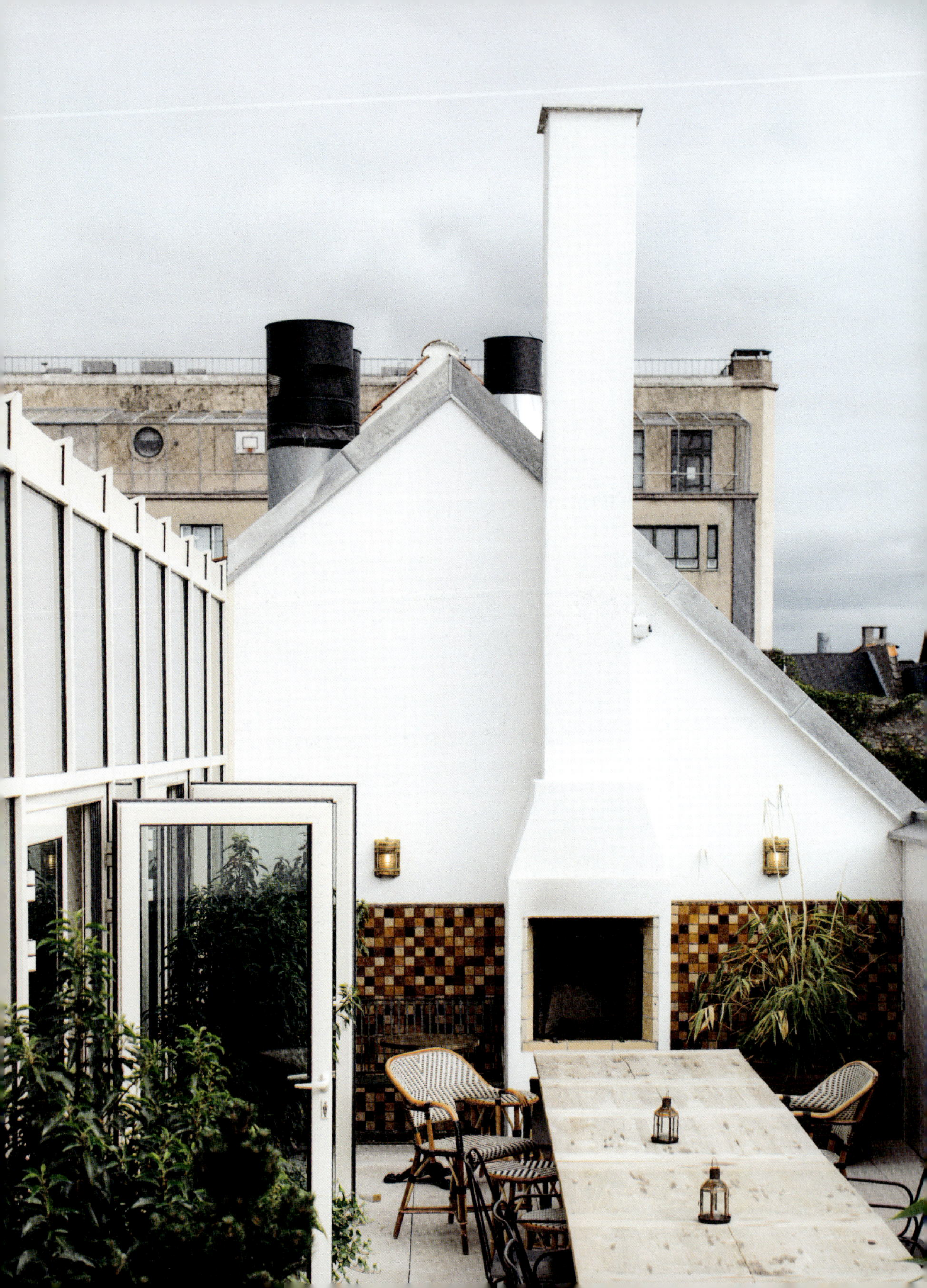

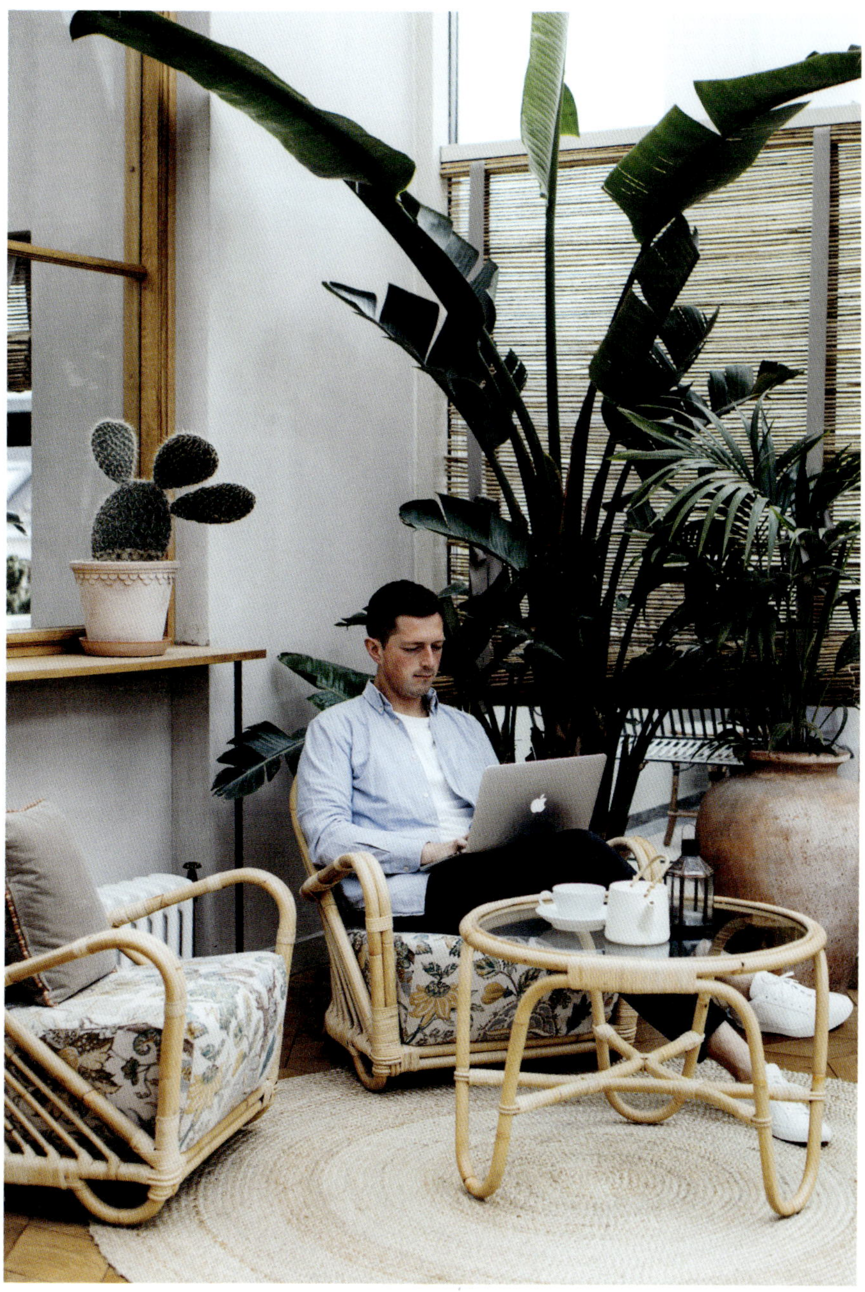

Thursday 6:55 PM

Relaxing and shutting down for the weekend

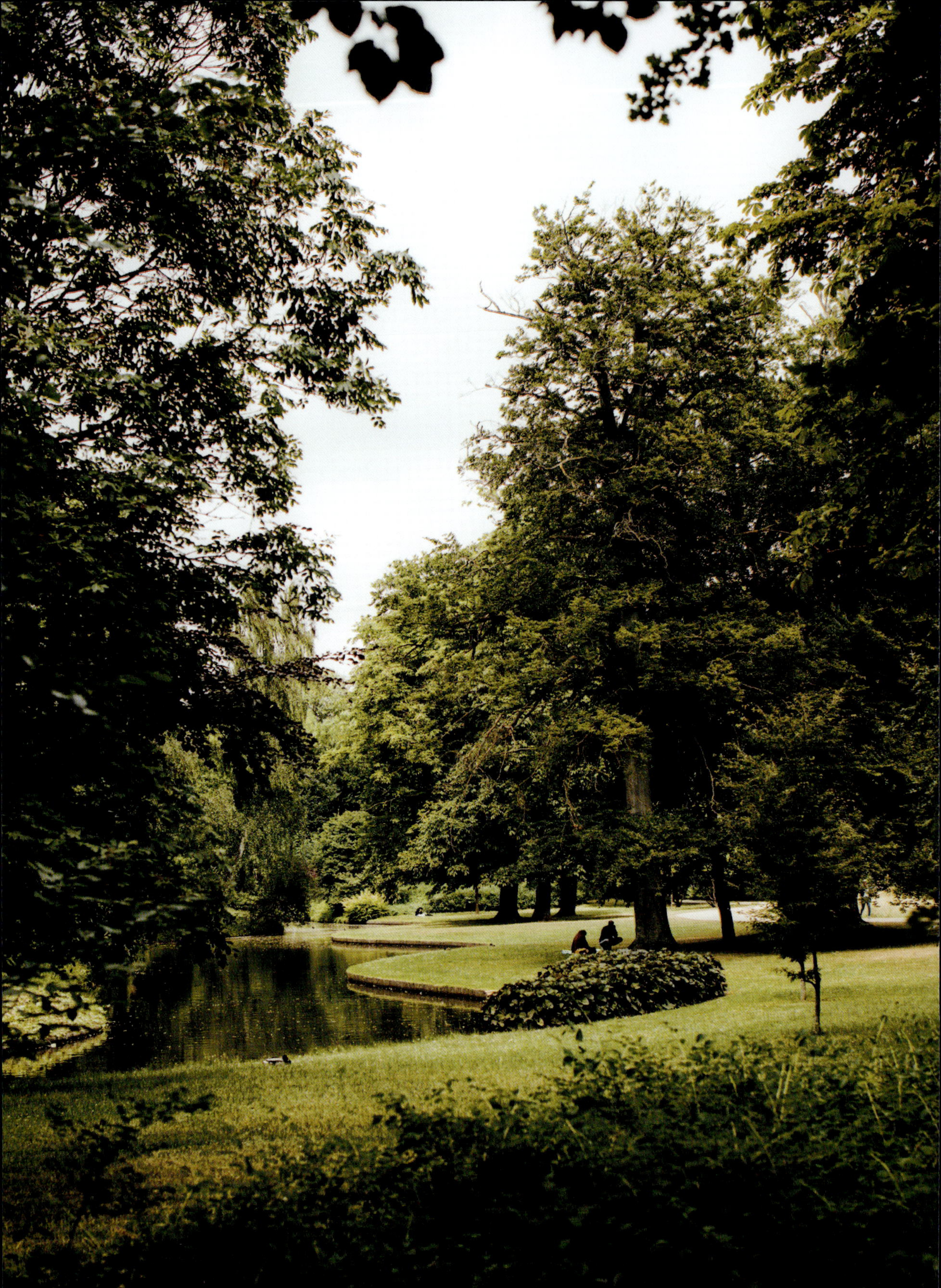

Friday

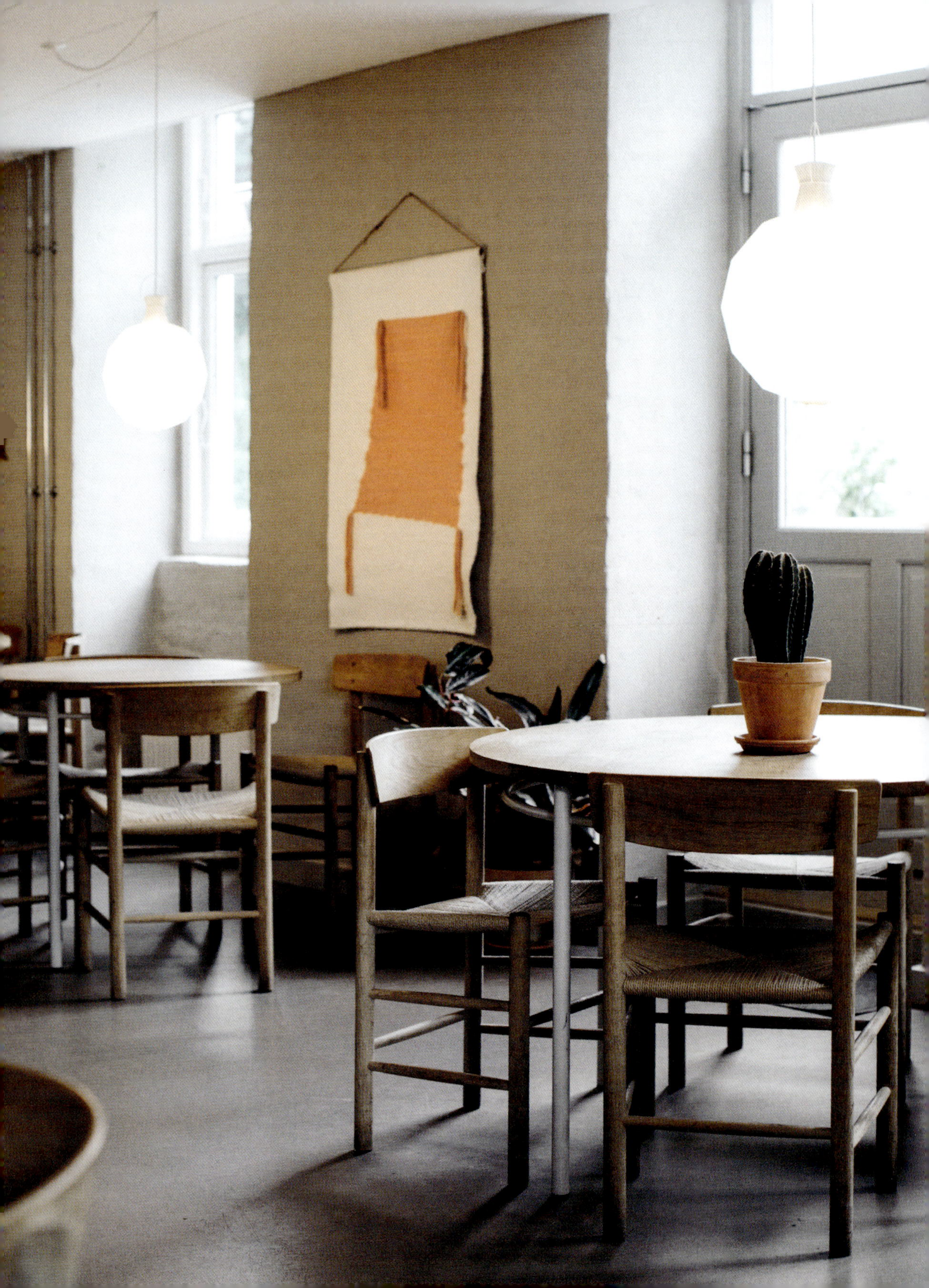

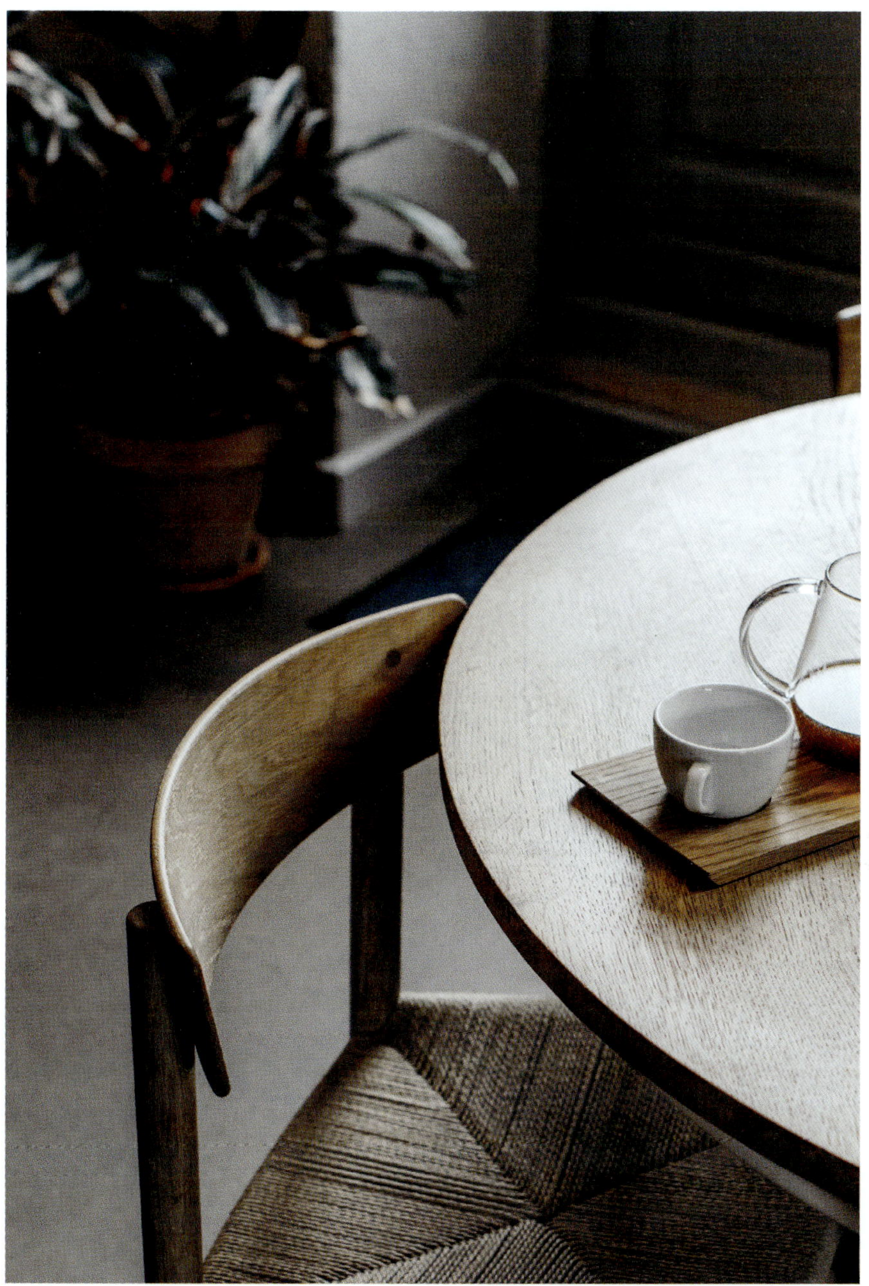

Friday 10:40 AM

Coffee Collective, Jægersborggade

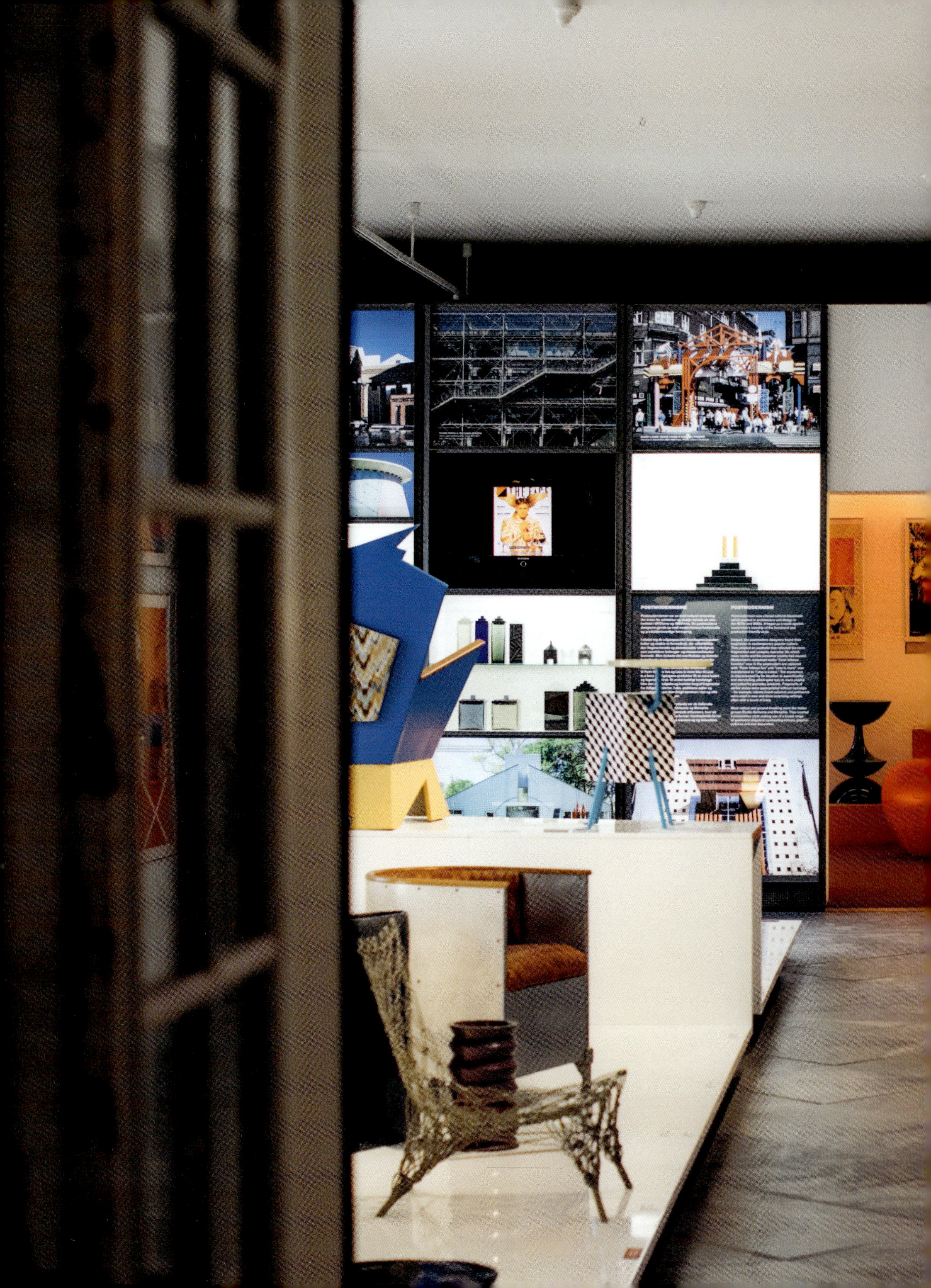

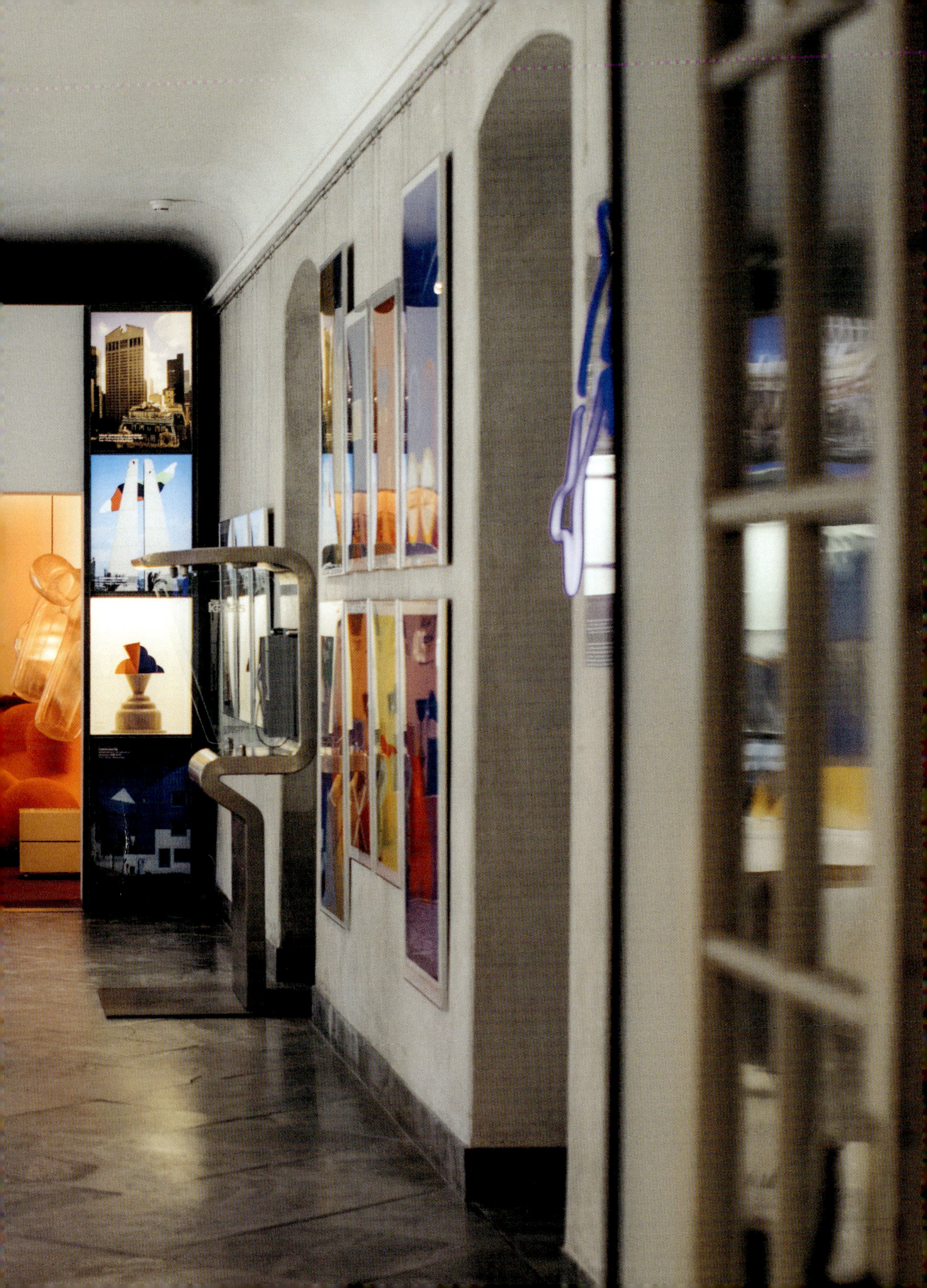

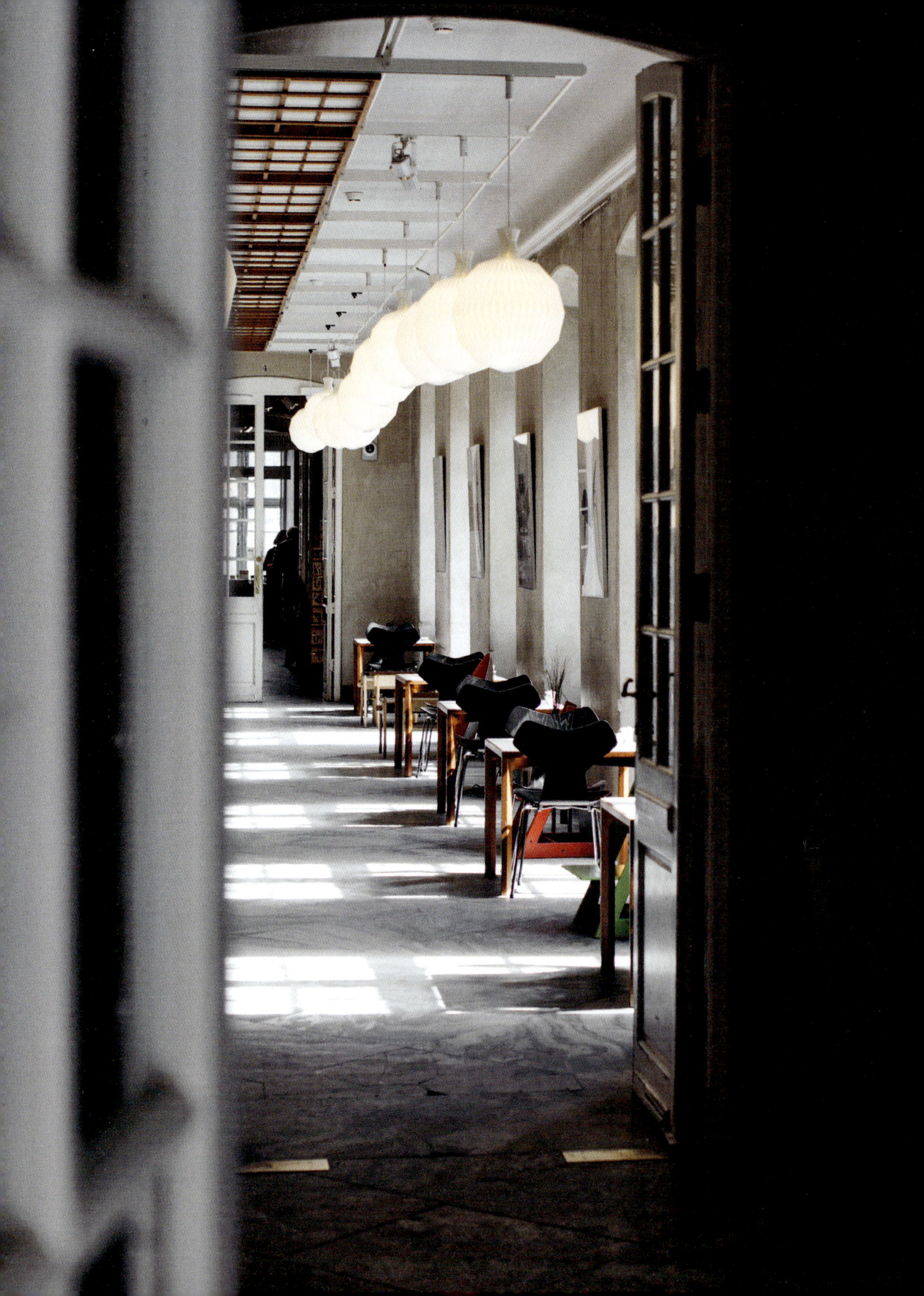

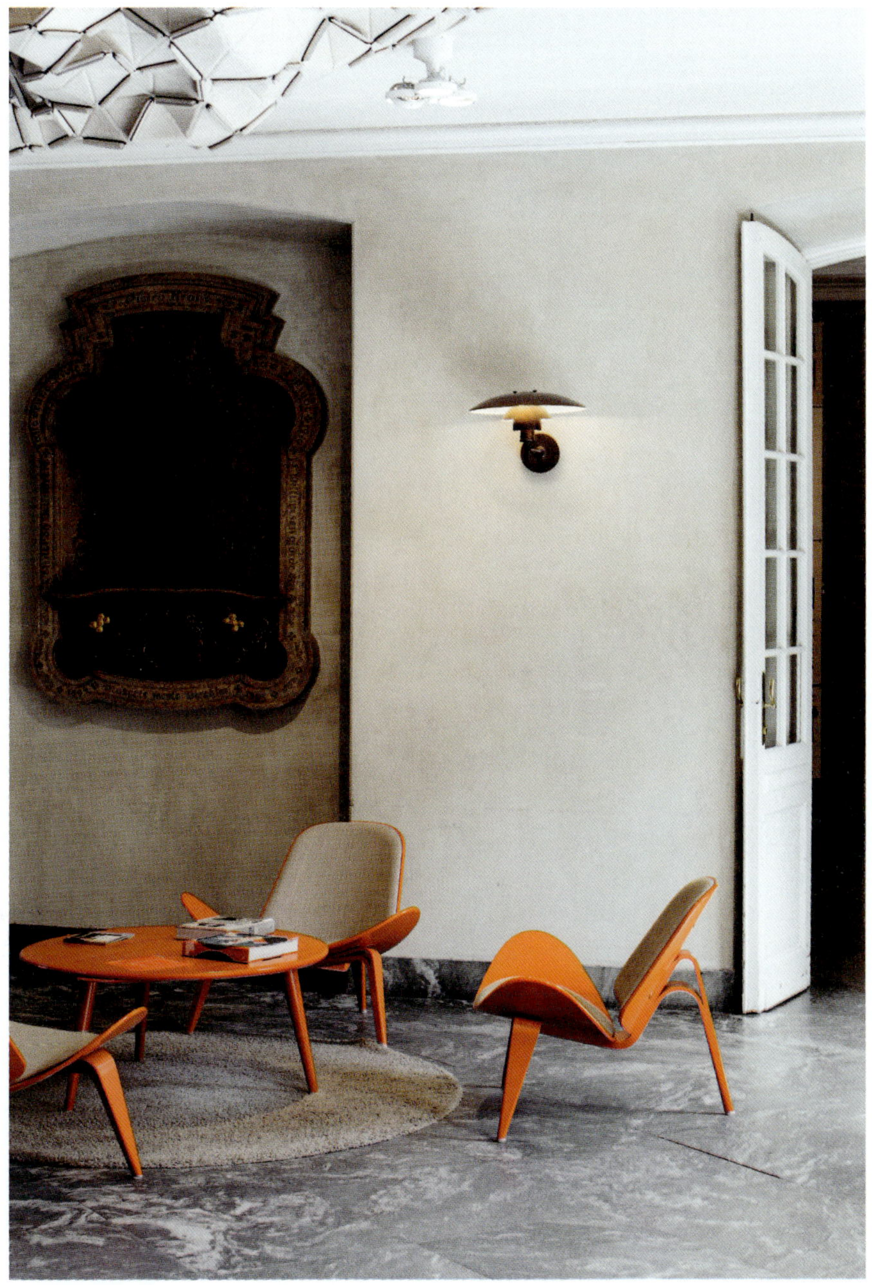

Friday 12:40 PM

Danish Museum of Art & Design

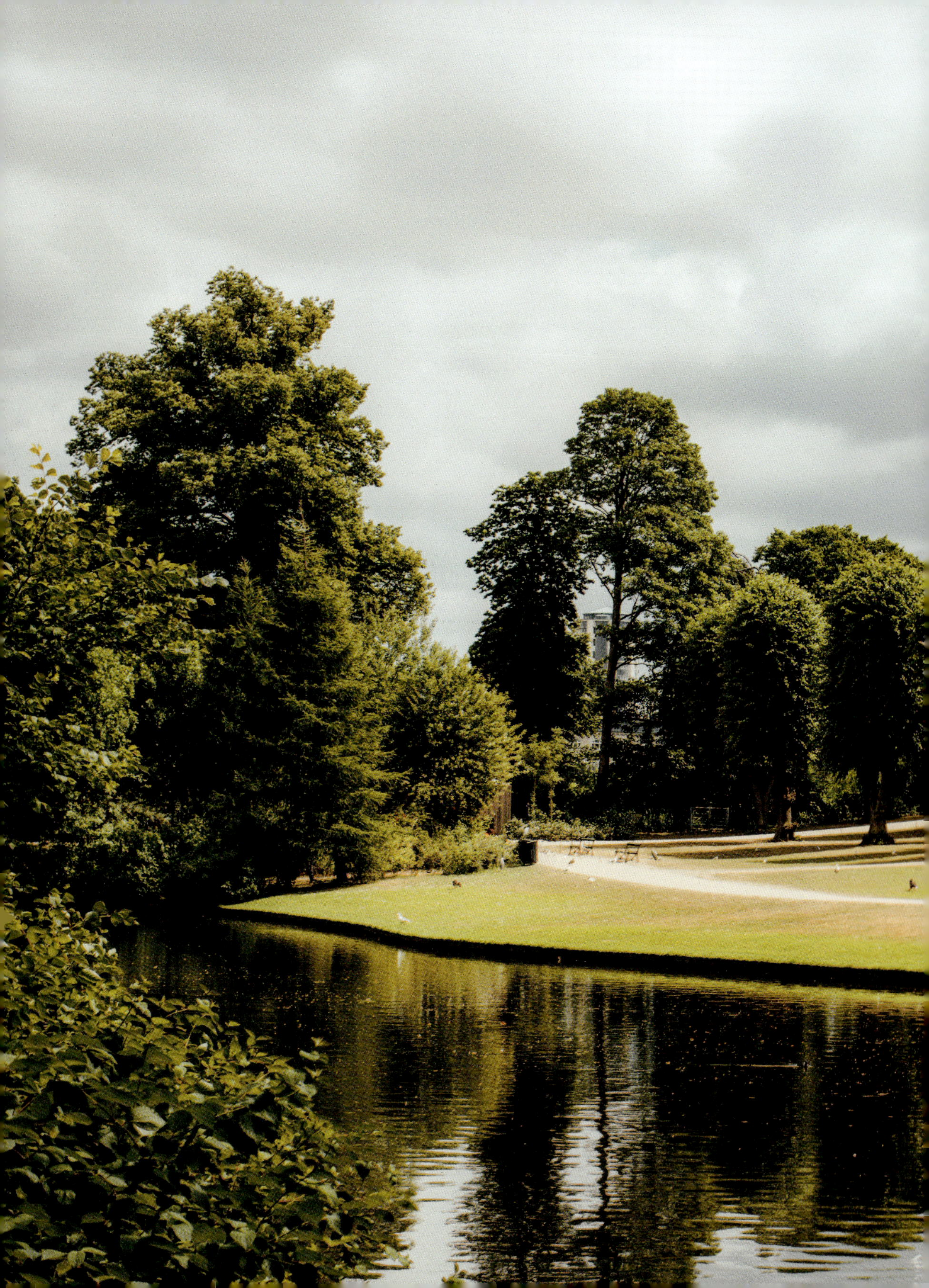

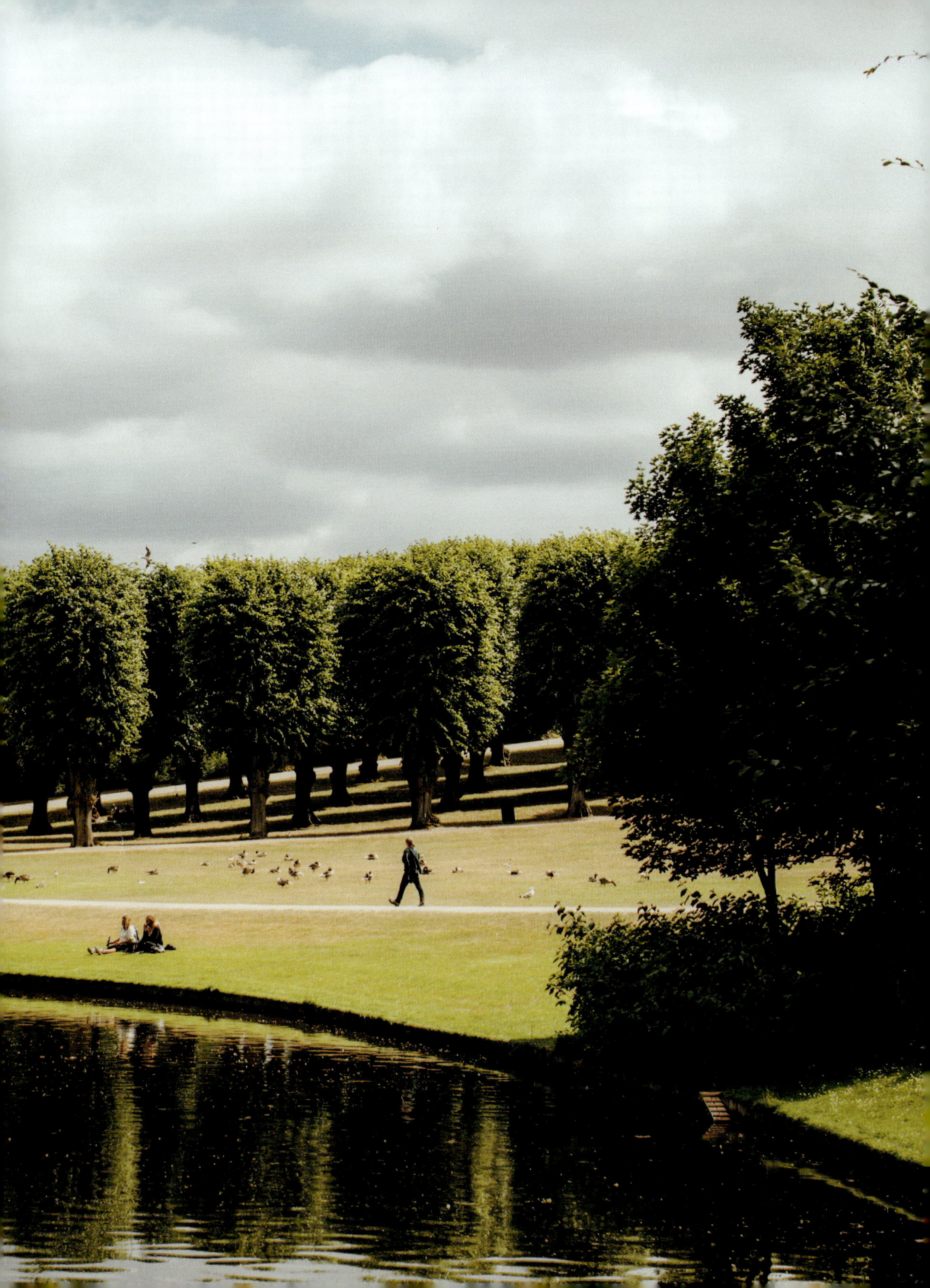

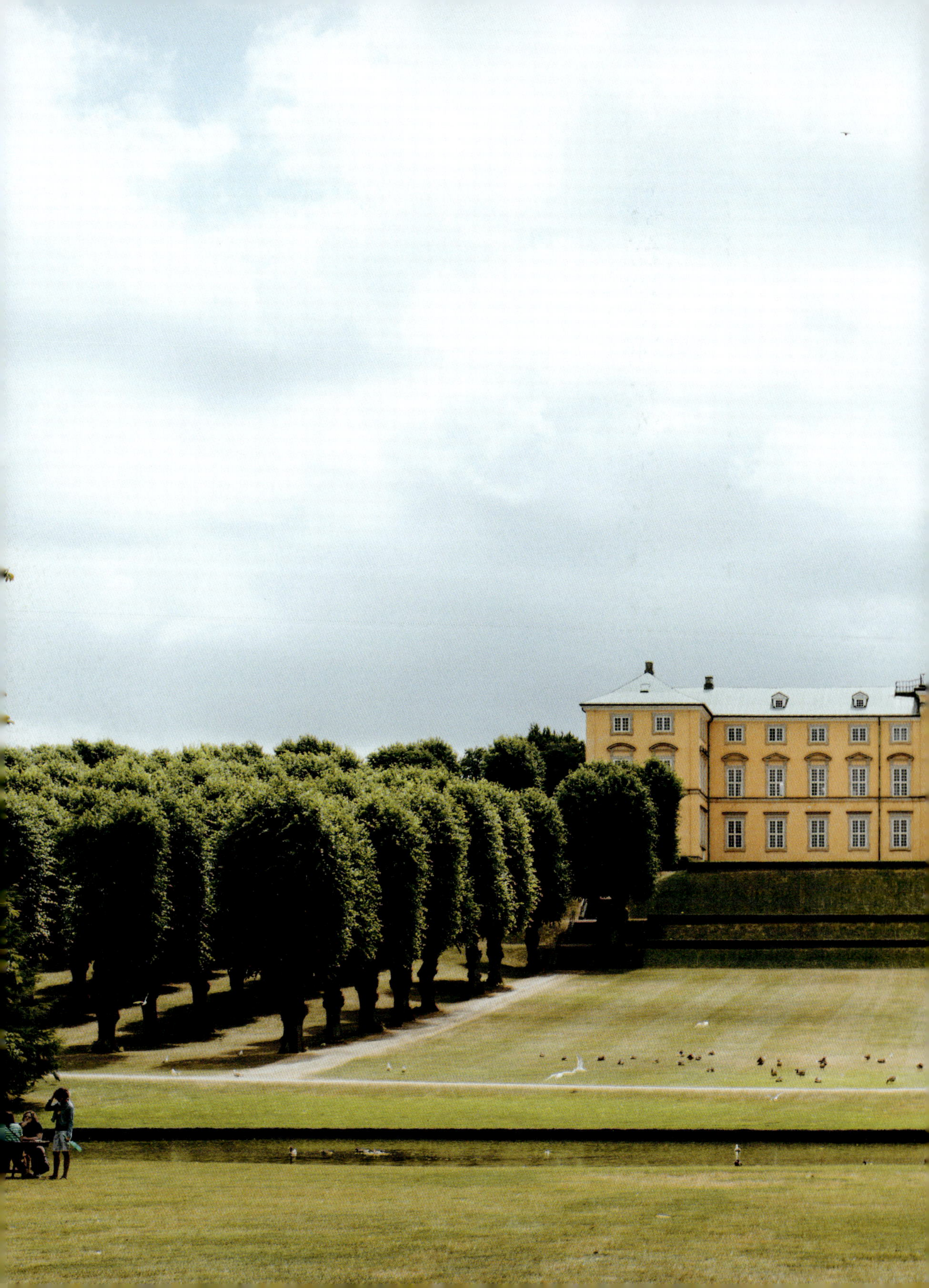

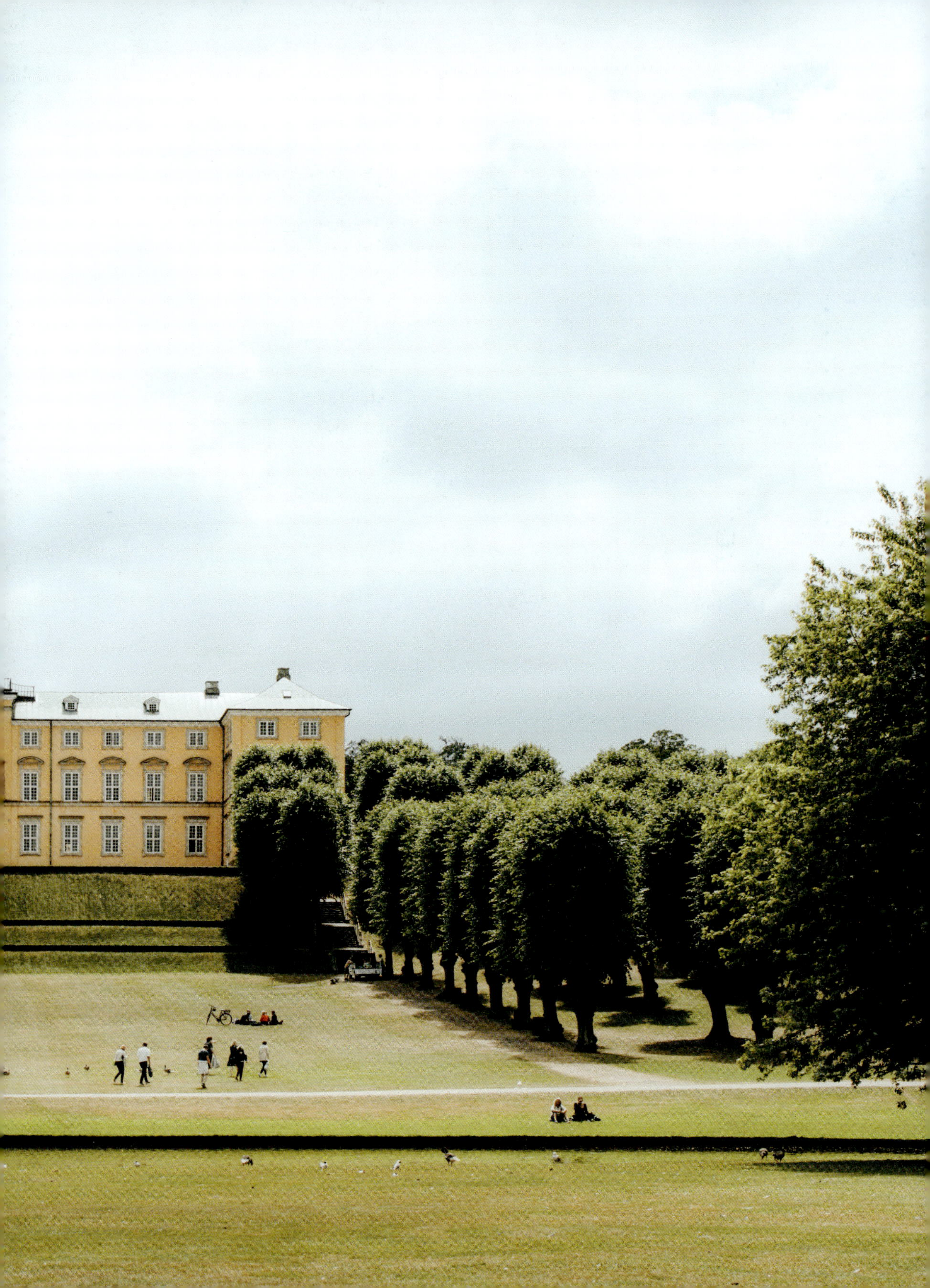

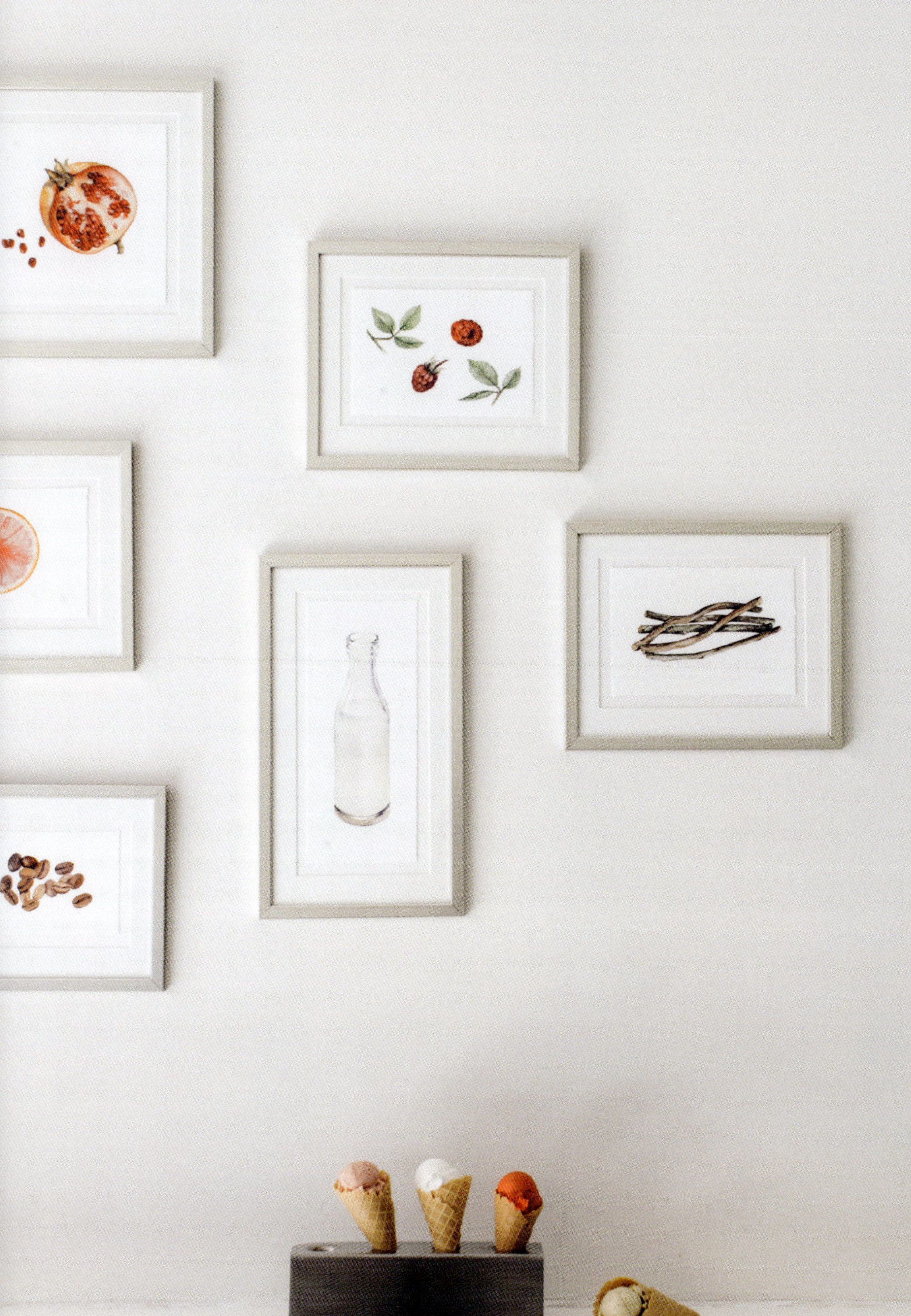

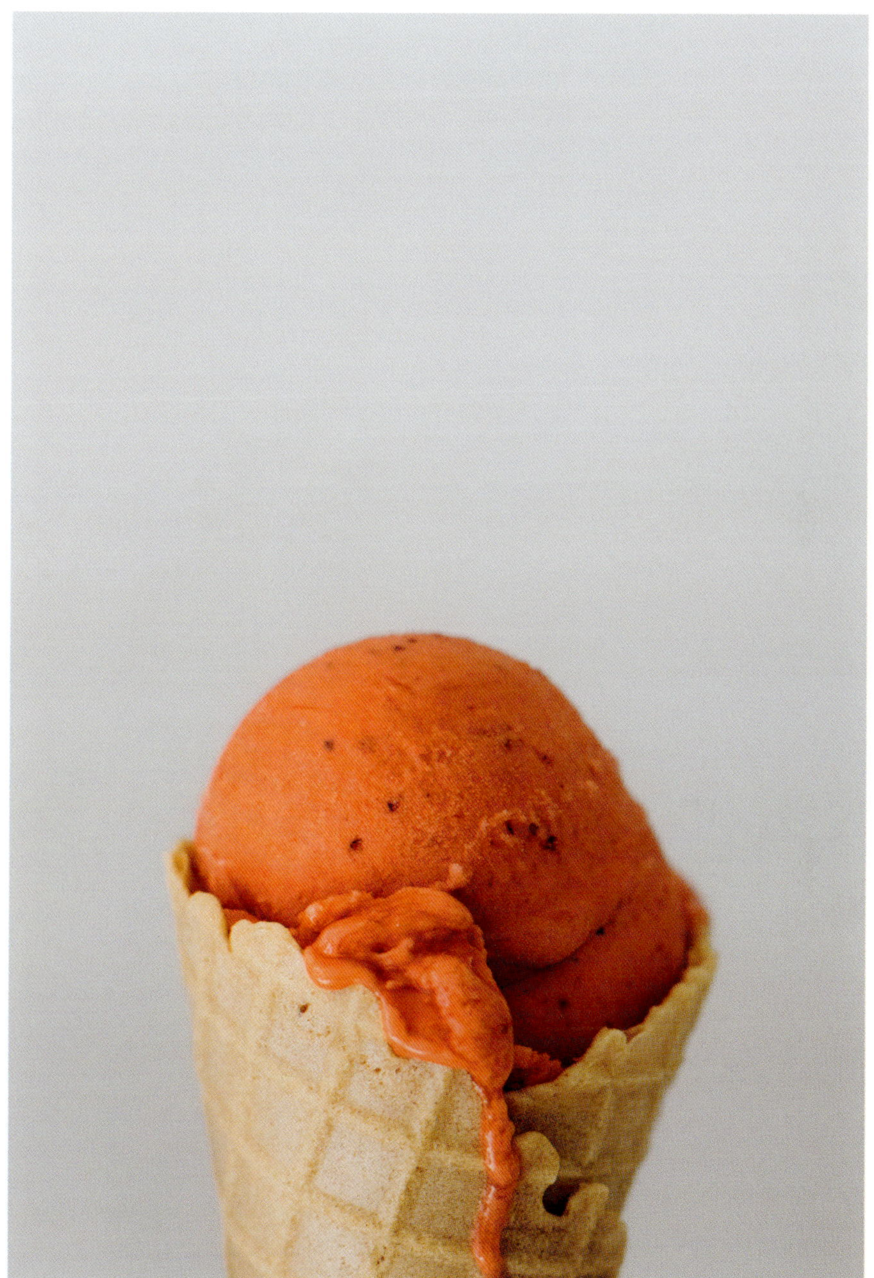

Friday 3:06 PM

A cooling treat at Østerberg Ice Cream

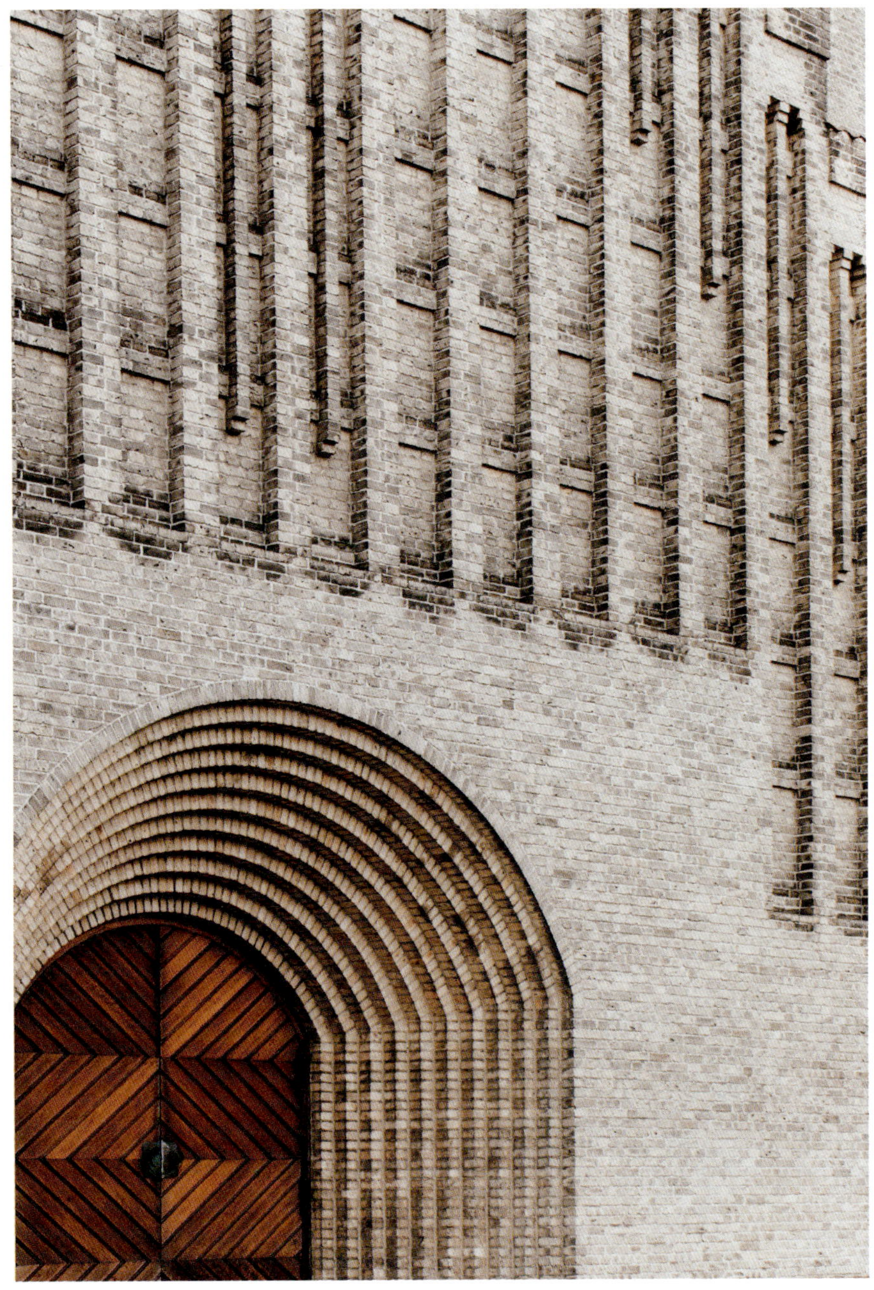

Grundtvig's Church

Friday 4:20 PM

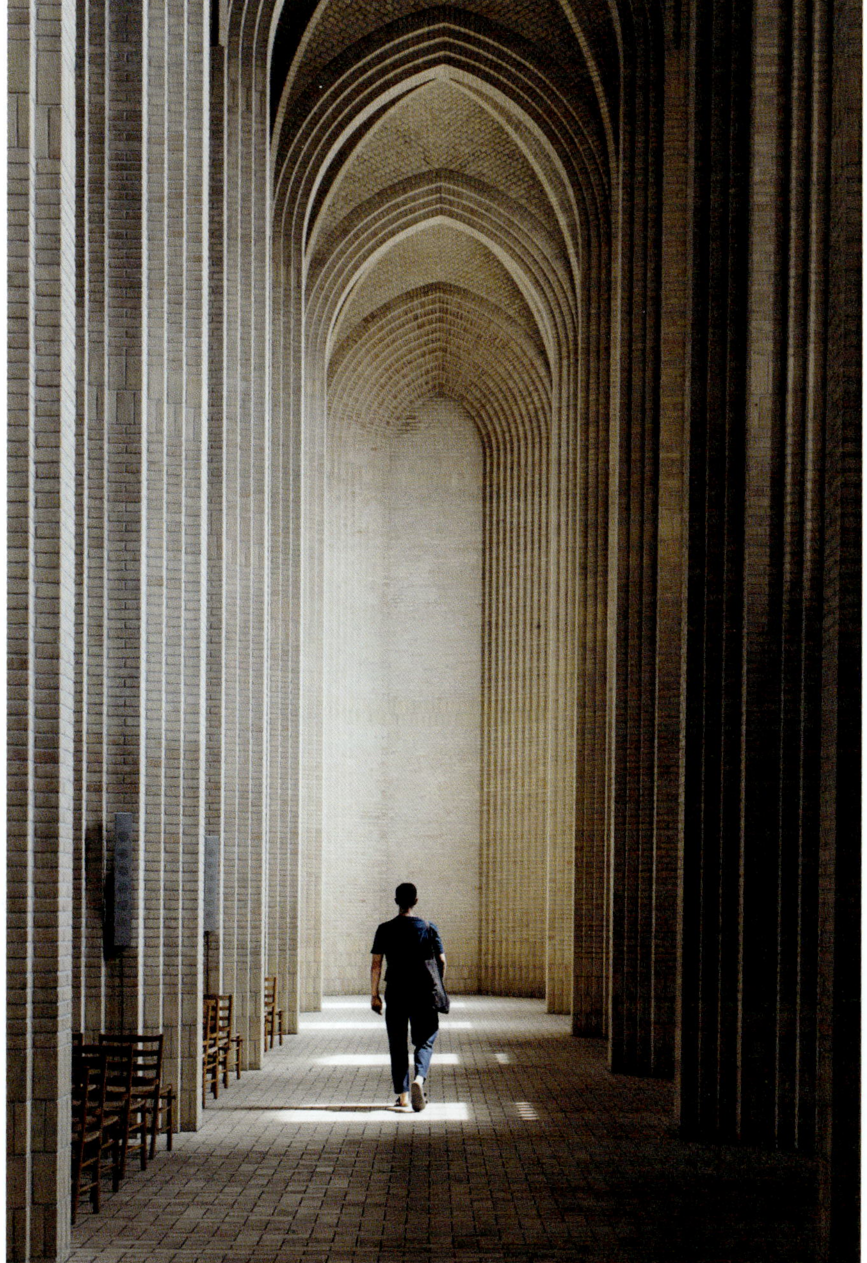

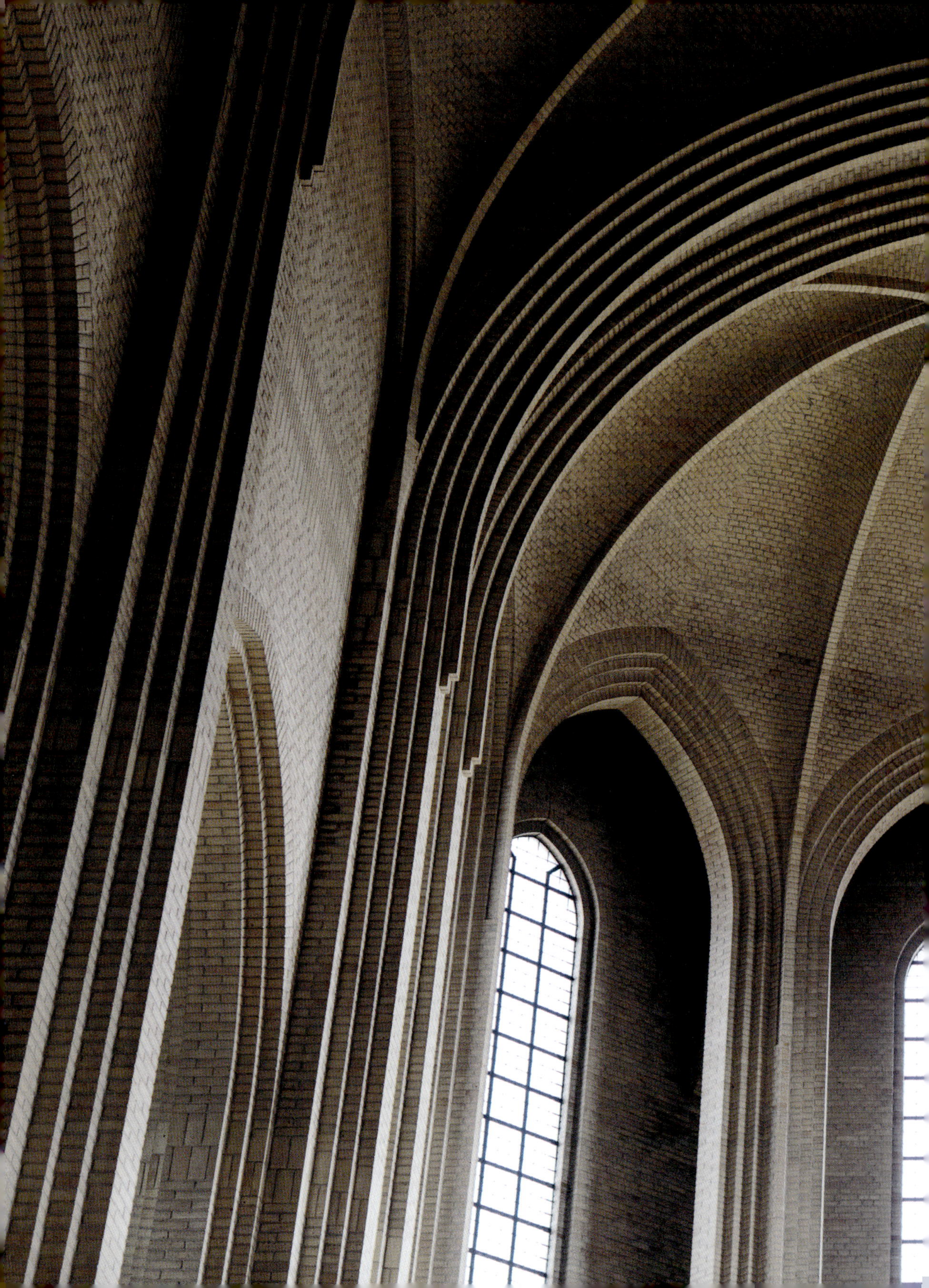

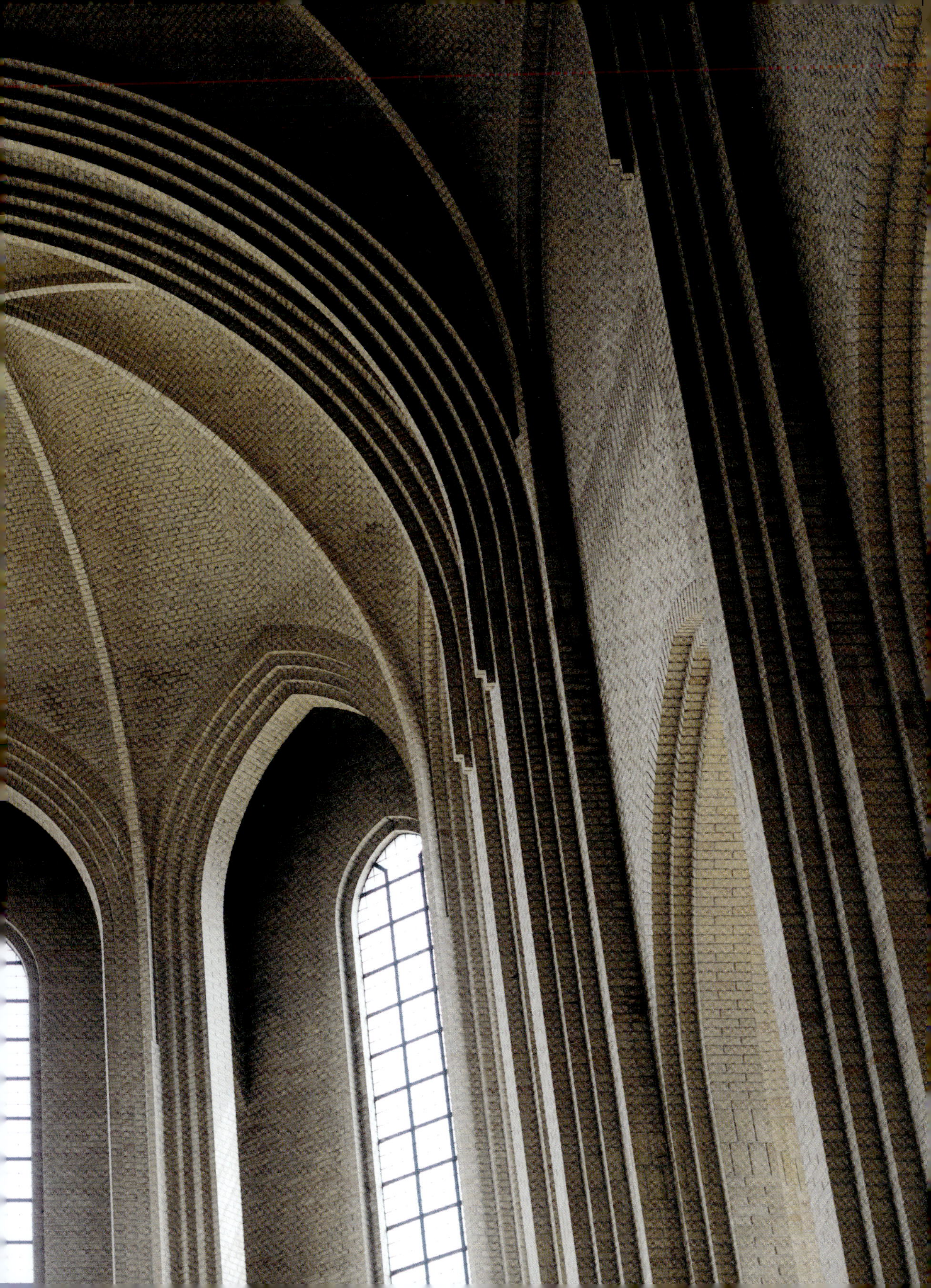

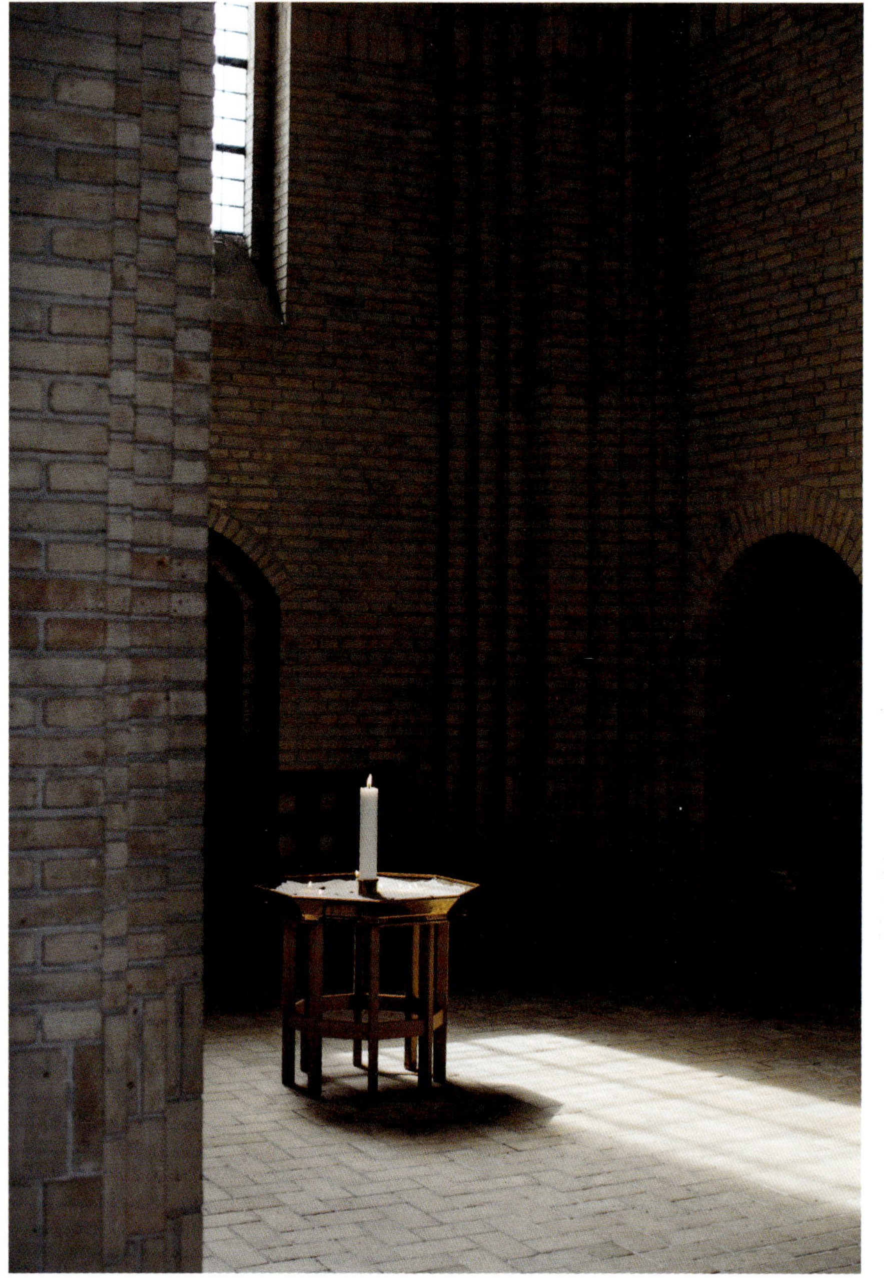

Cascading brickwork and quiet spaces

Friday 4:39 PM

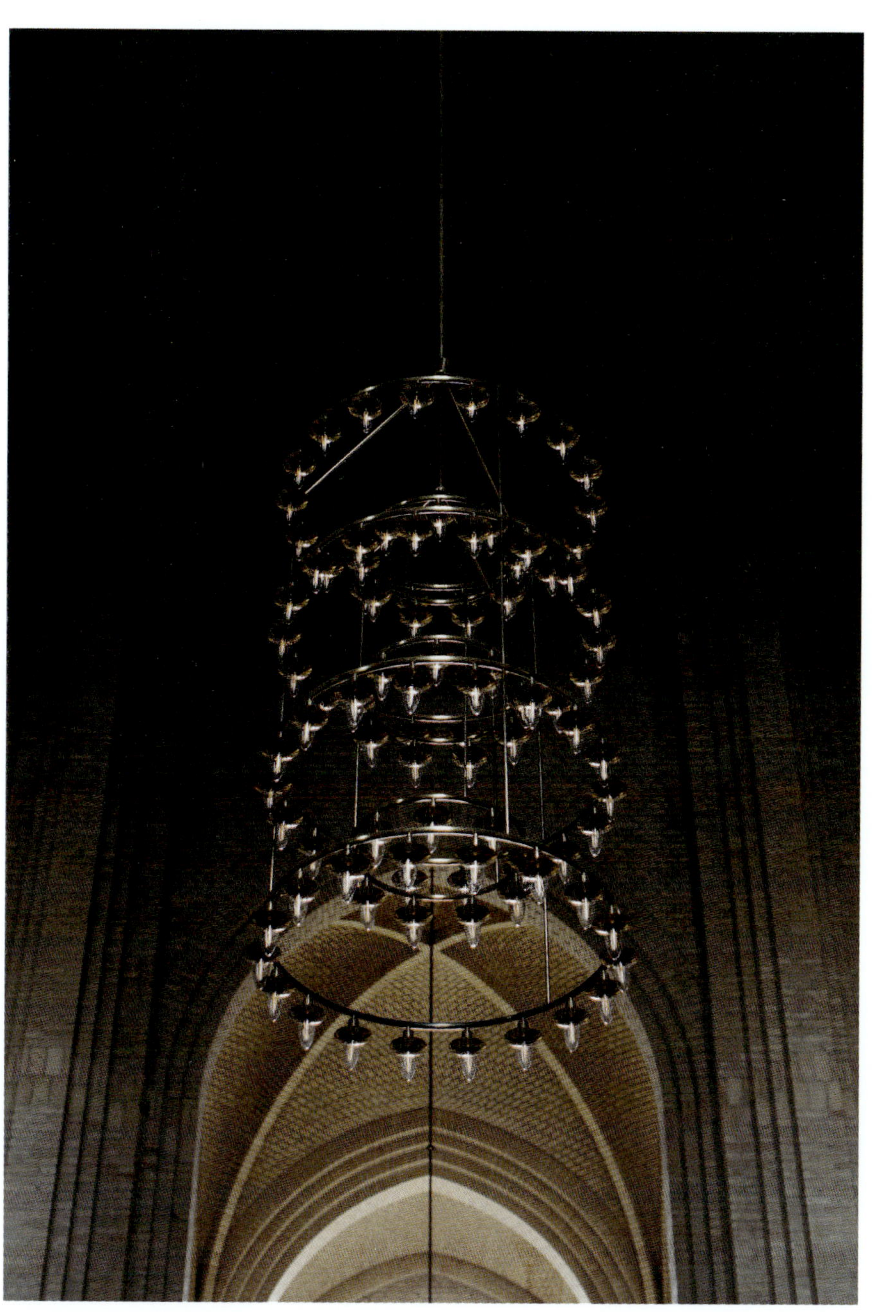

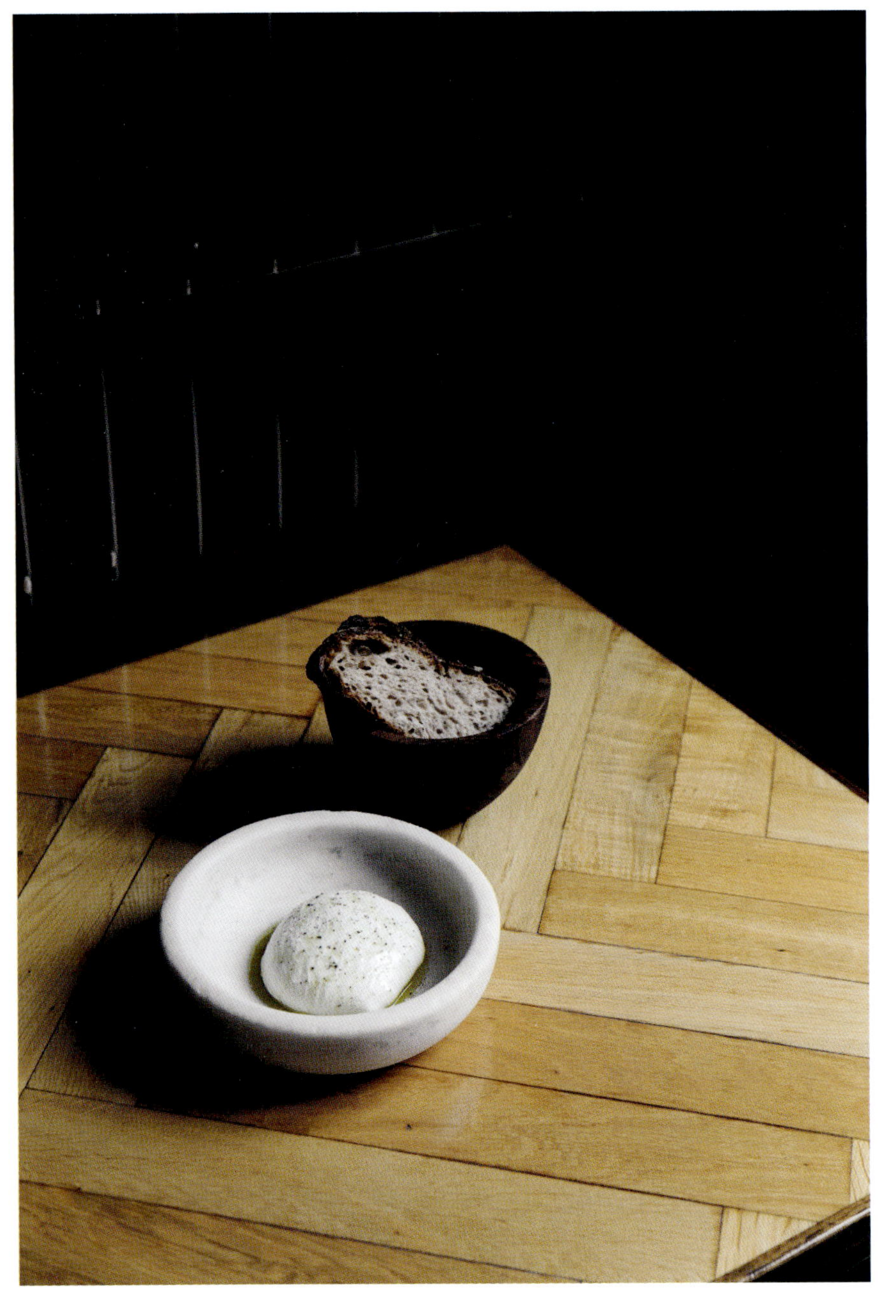

Dinner at BÆST

Friday 7:45 PM

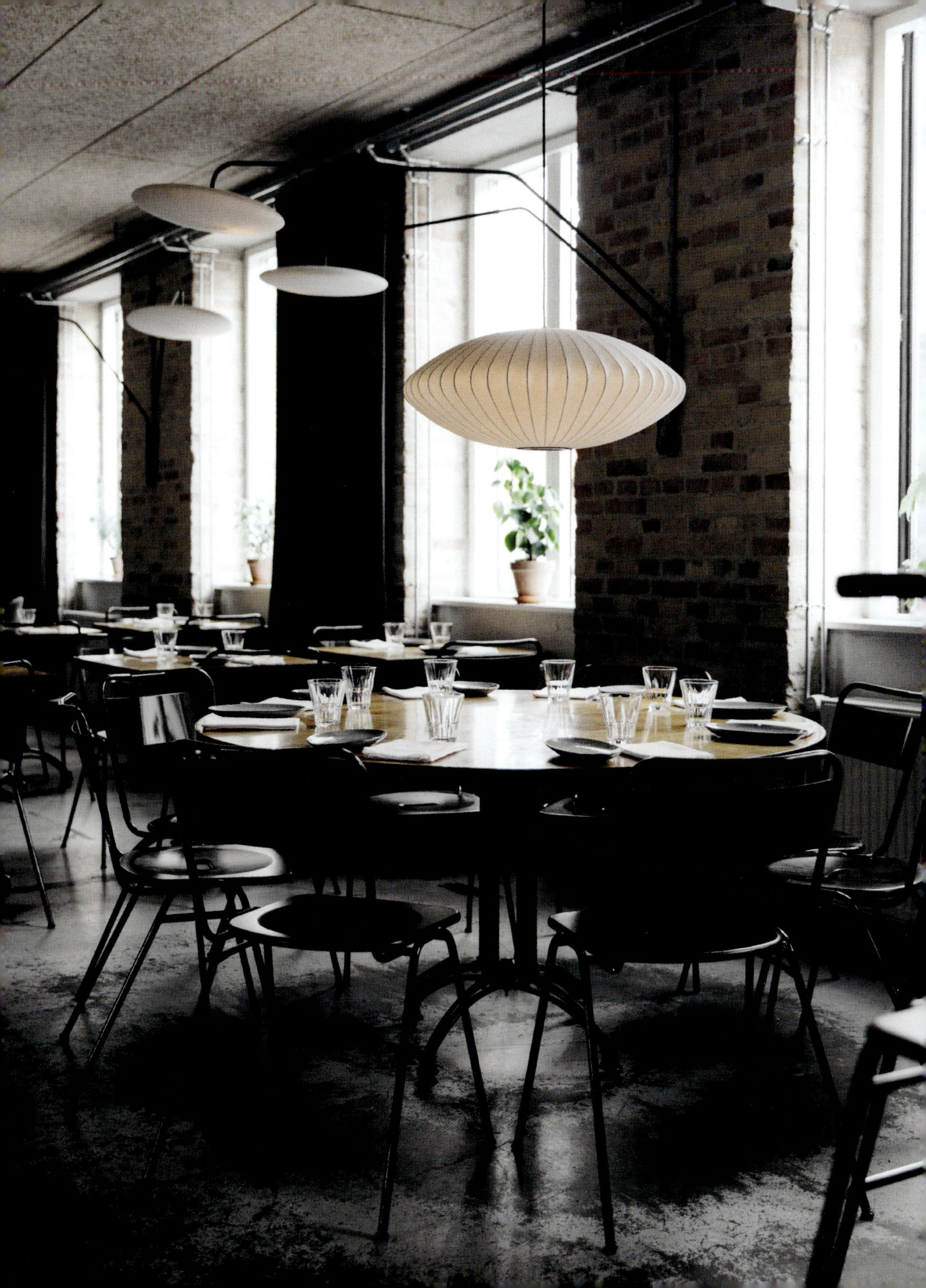

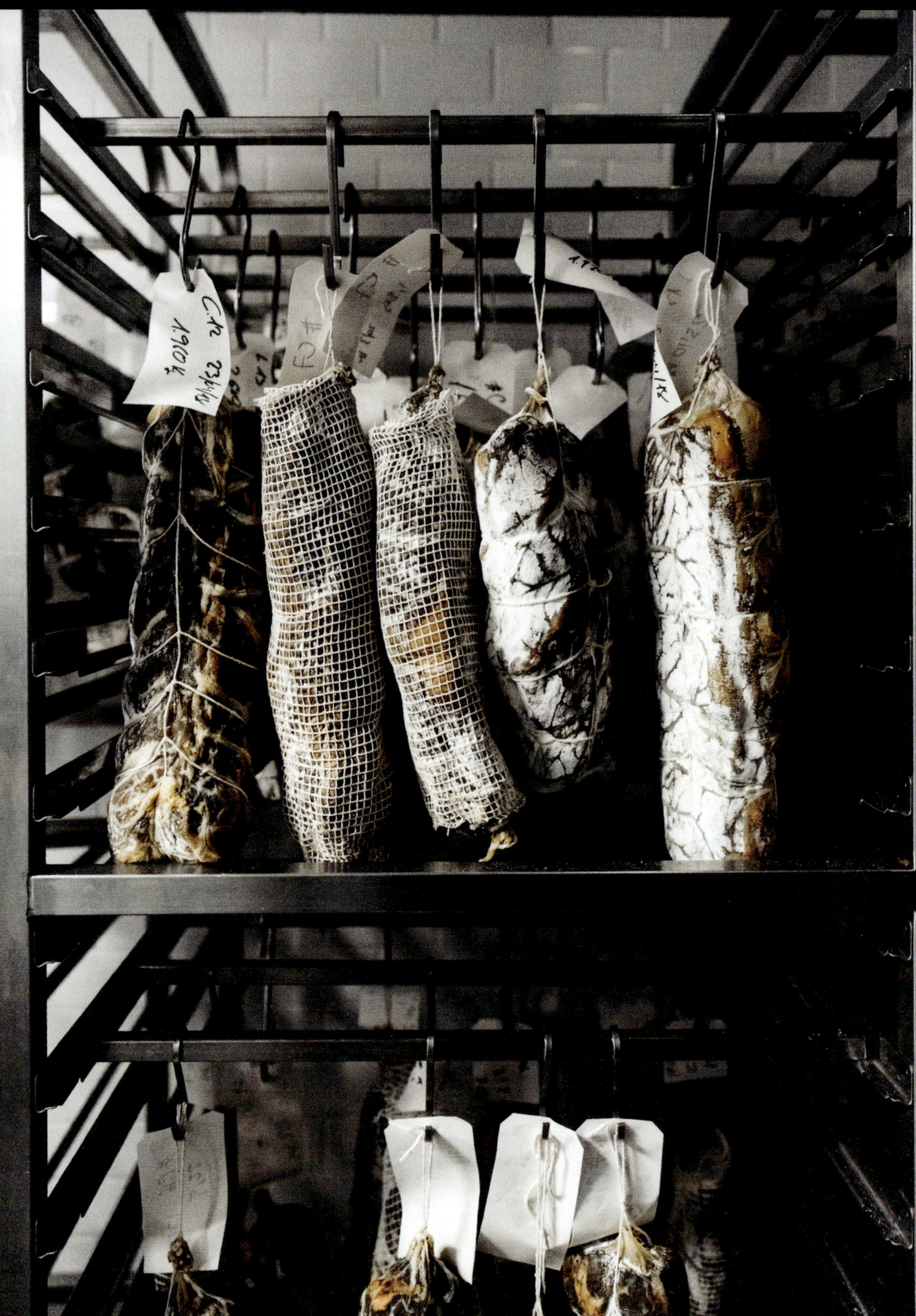

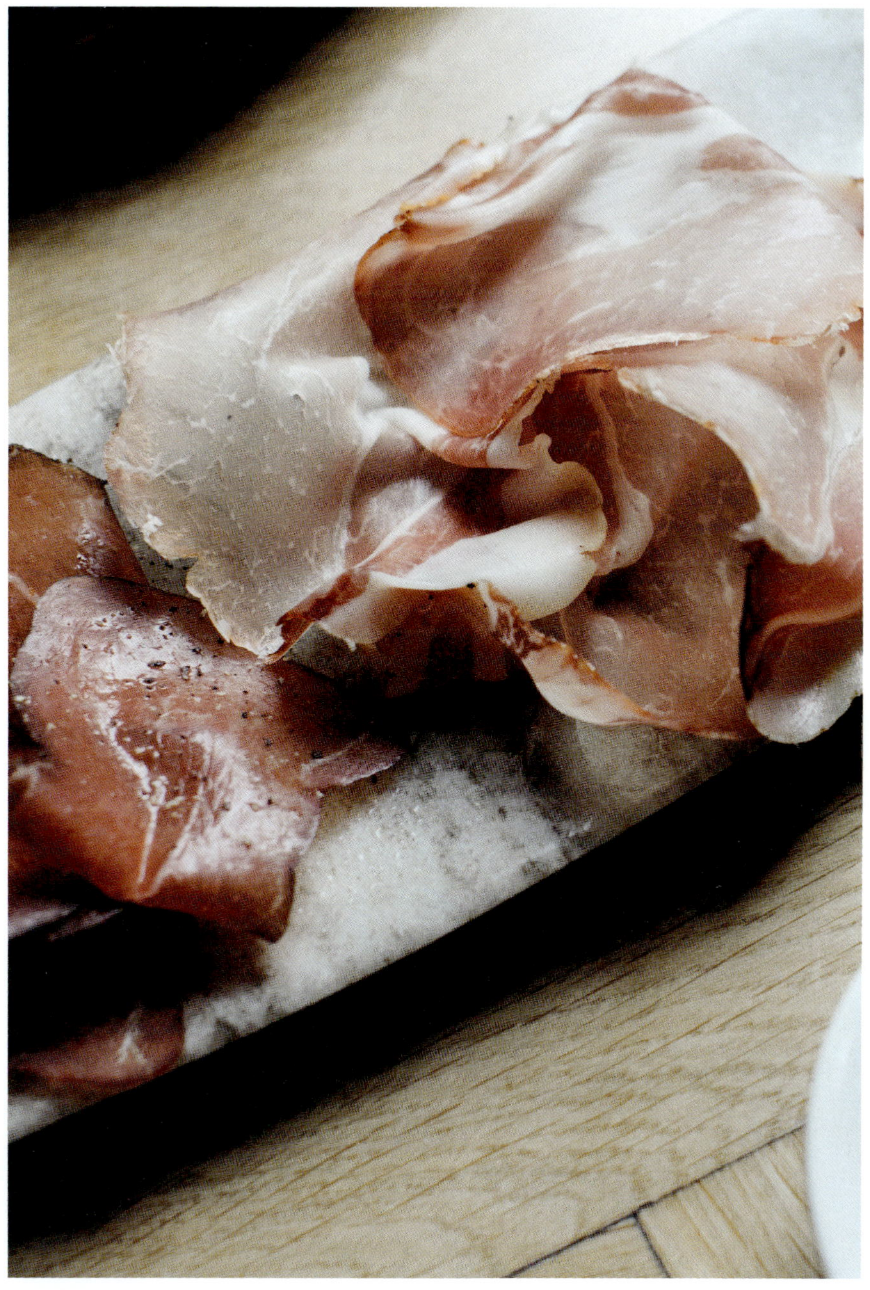

Friday 7:56 PM

Finest Danish ingredients sourced and stored

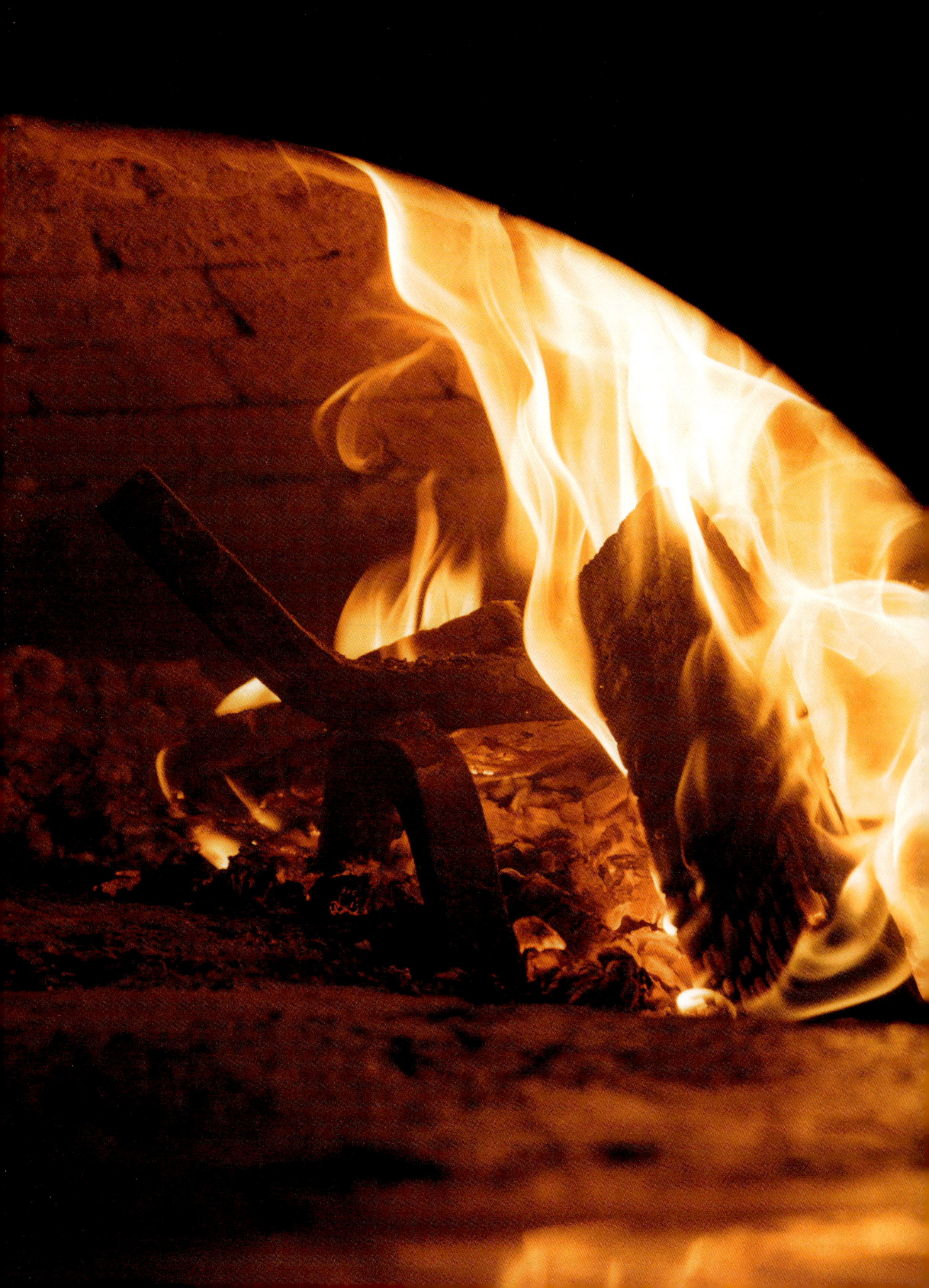

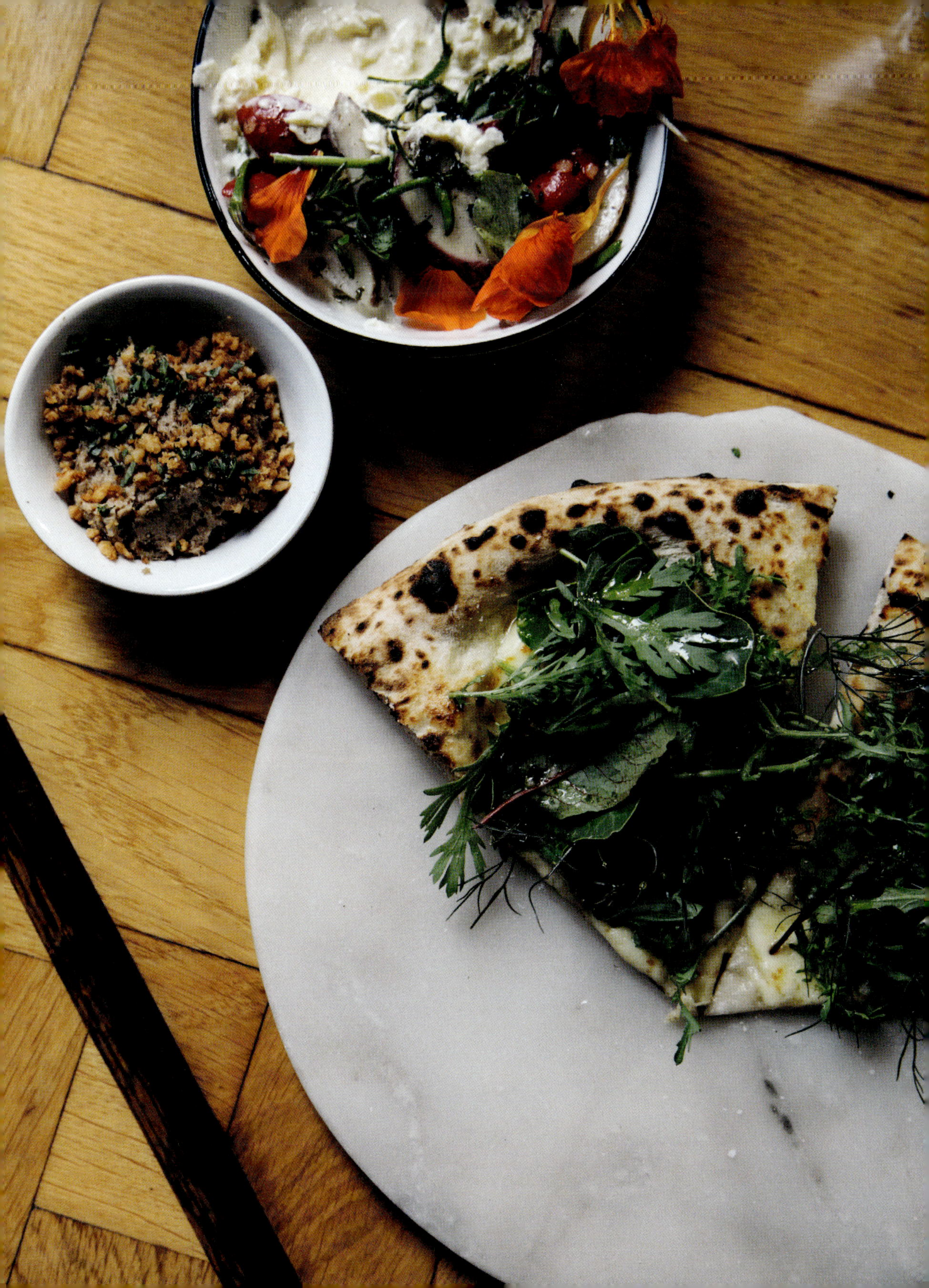

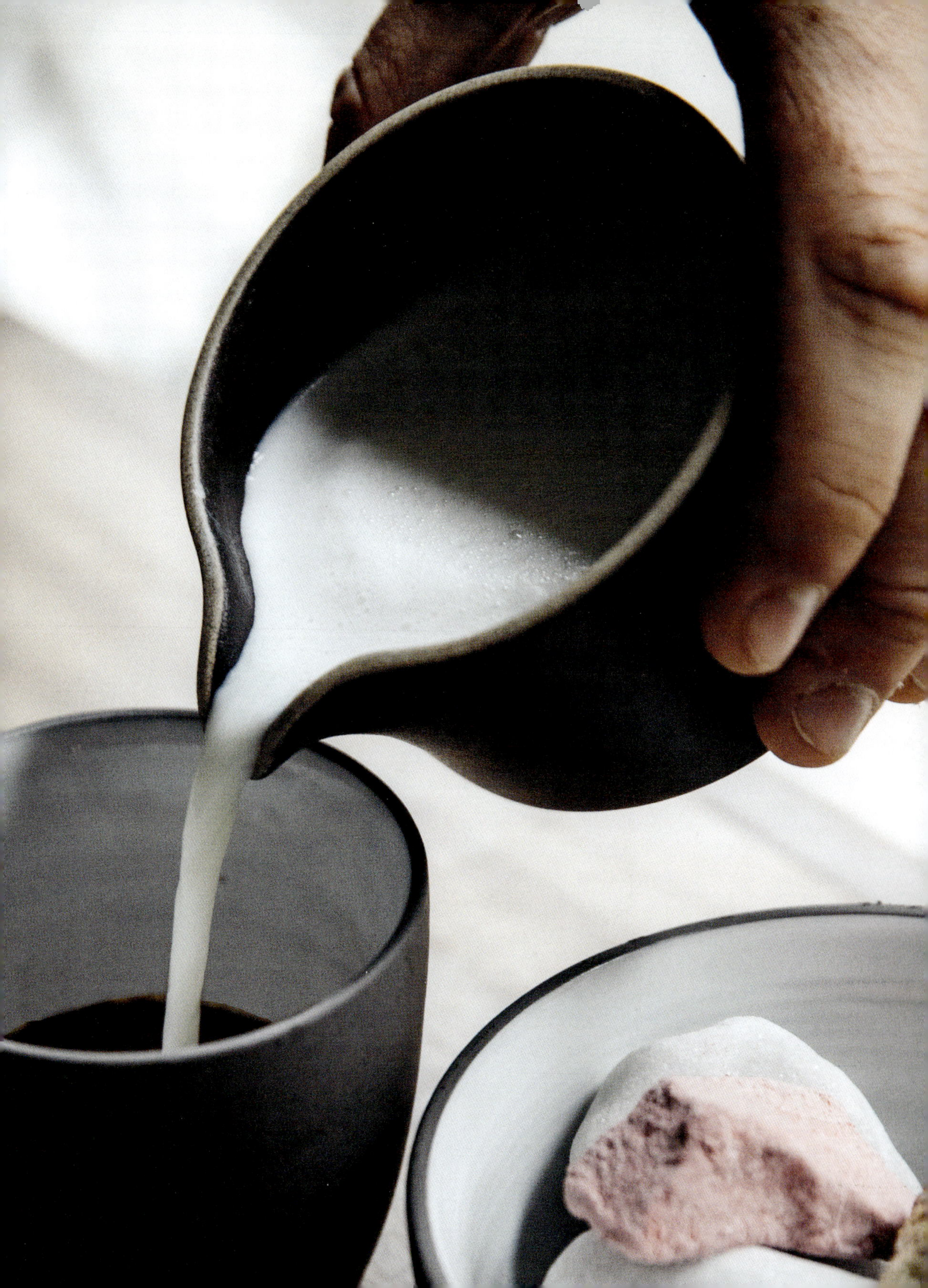

Saturday

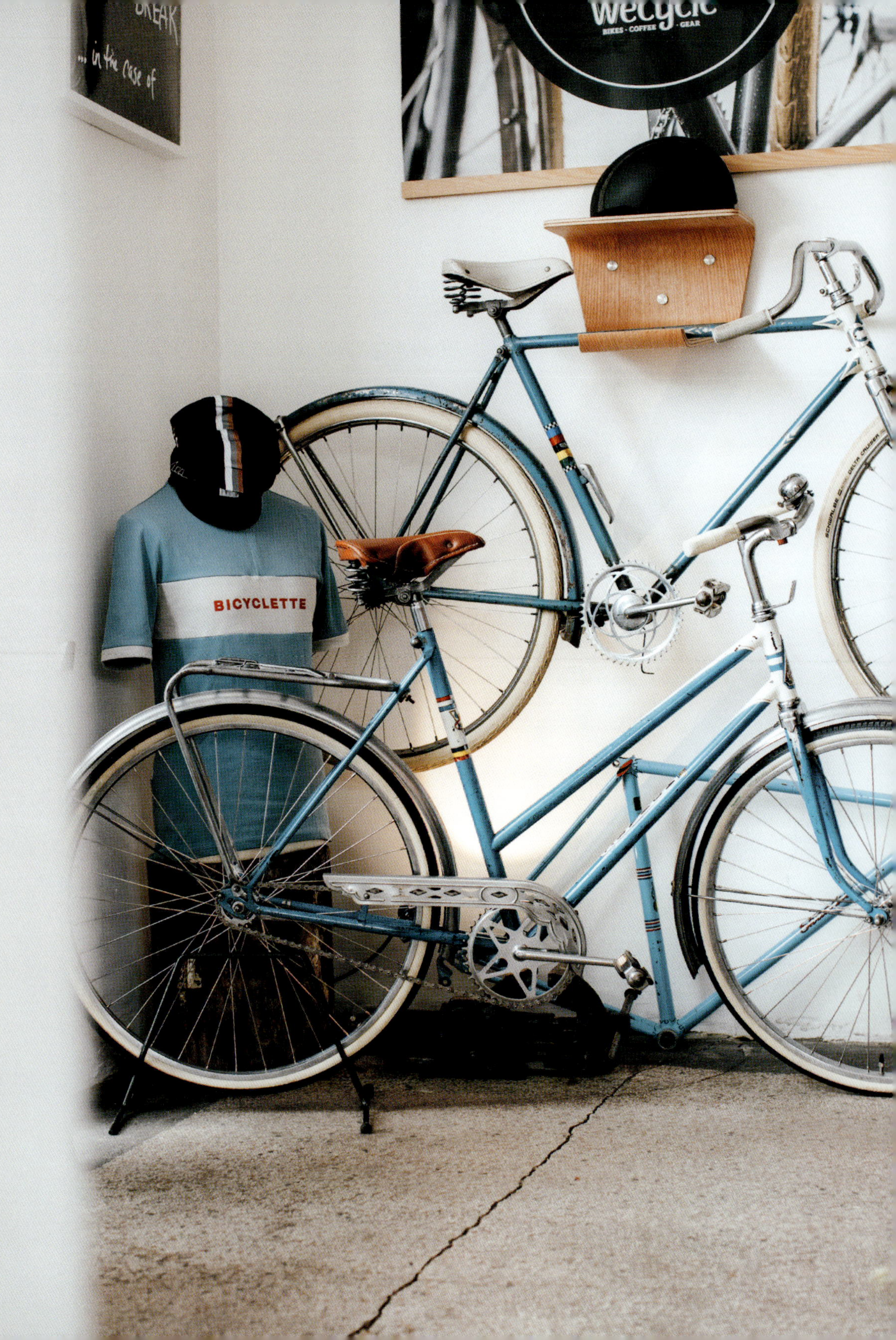
... in the case of
BIKES · COFFEE · GEAR
BICYCLETTE

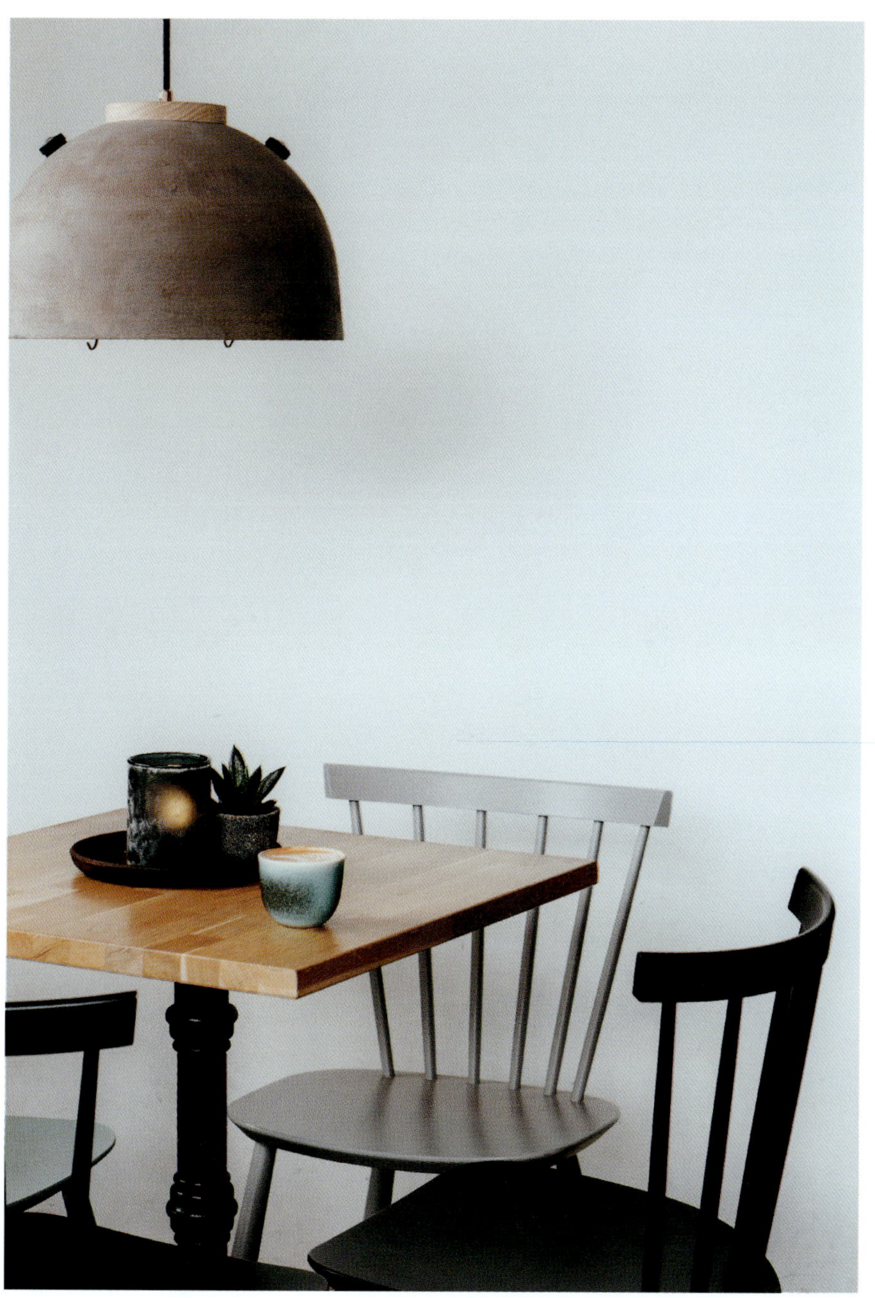

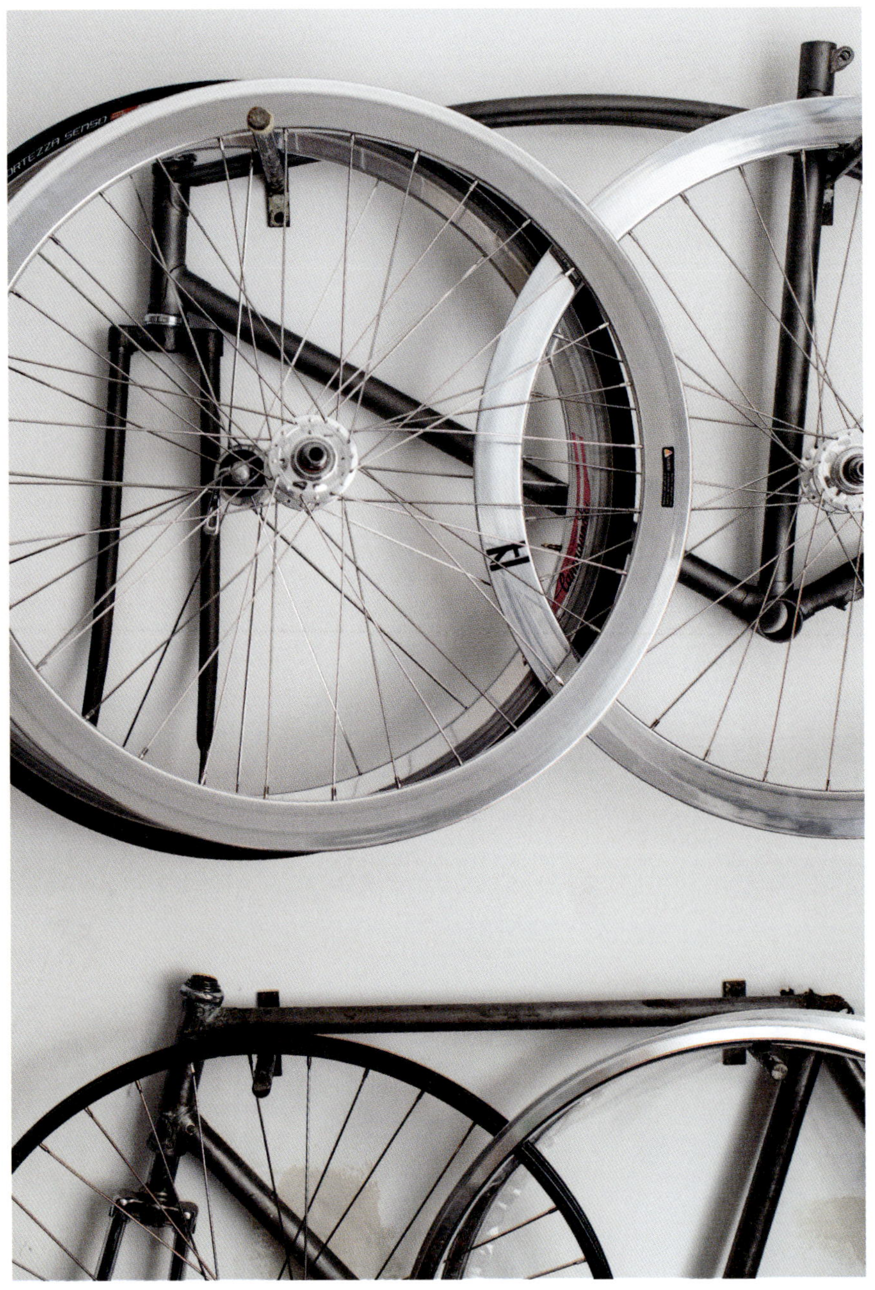

Wecycle Copenhagen Saturday 9:14 AM

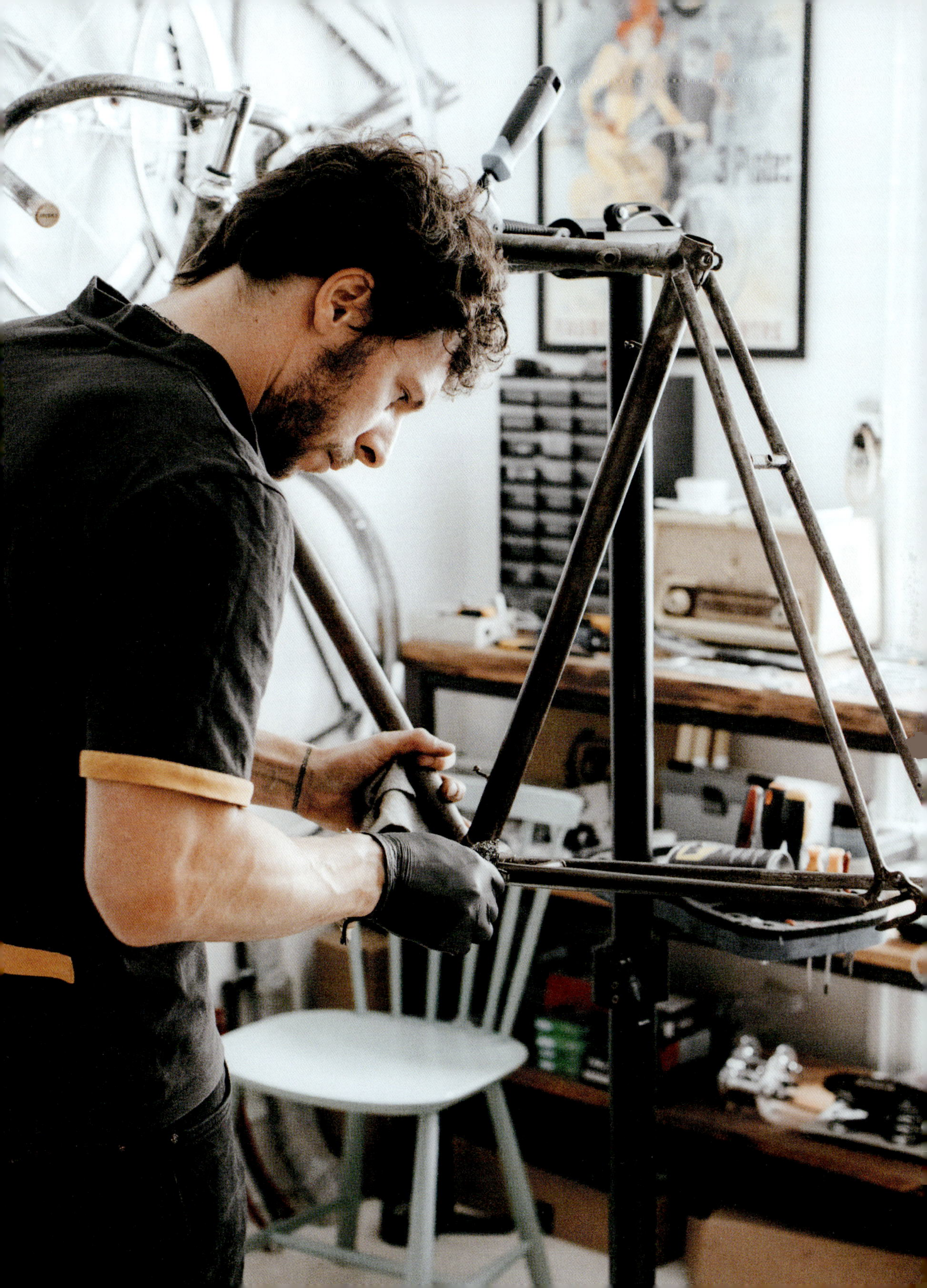

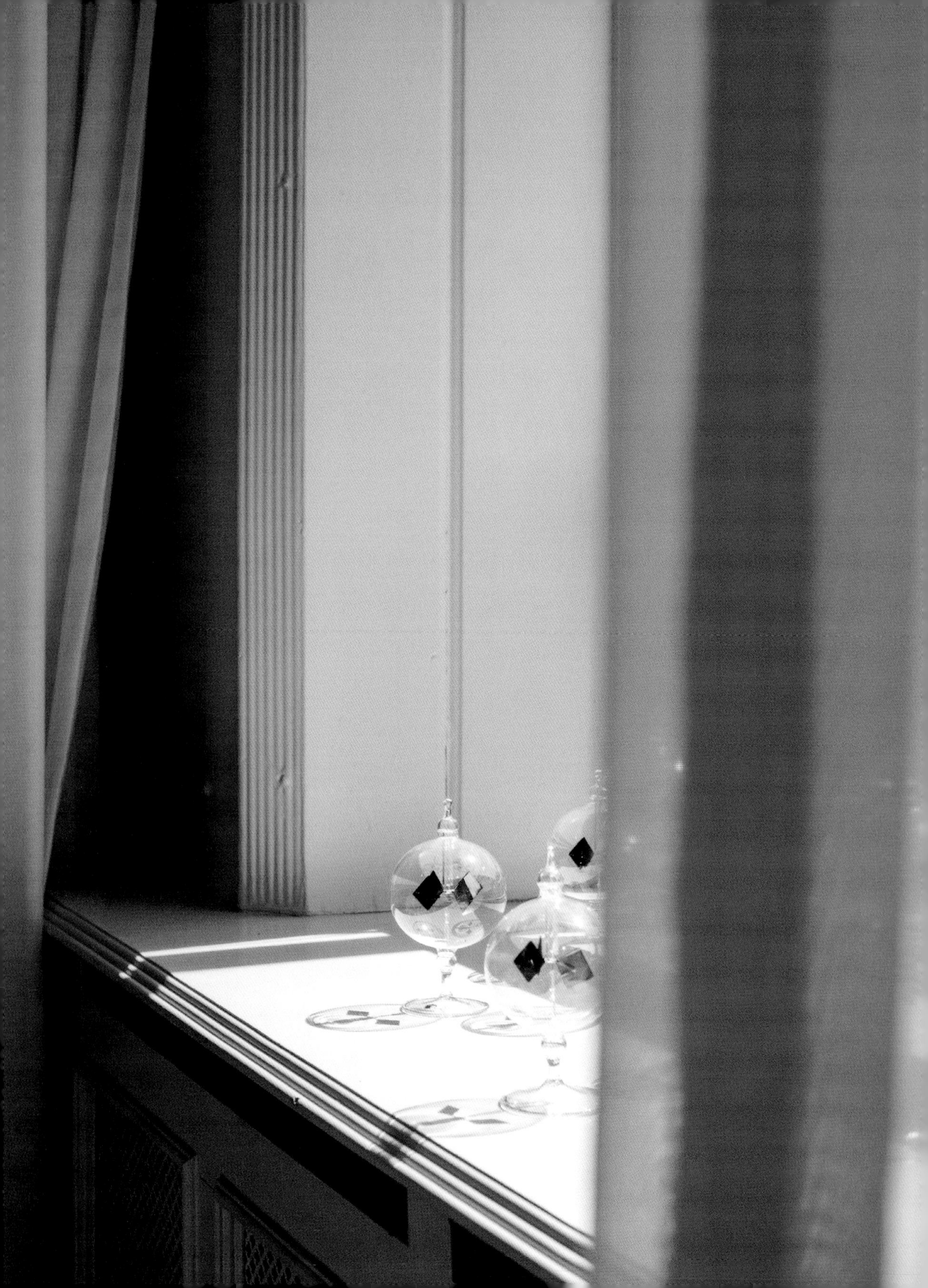

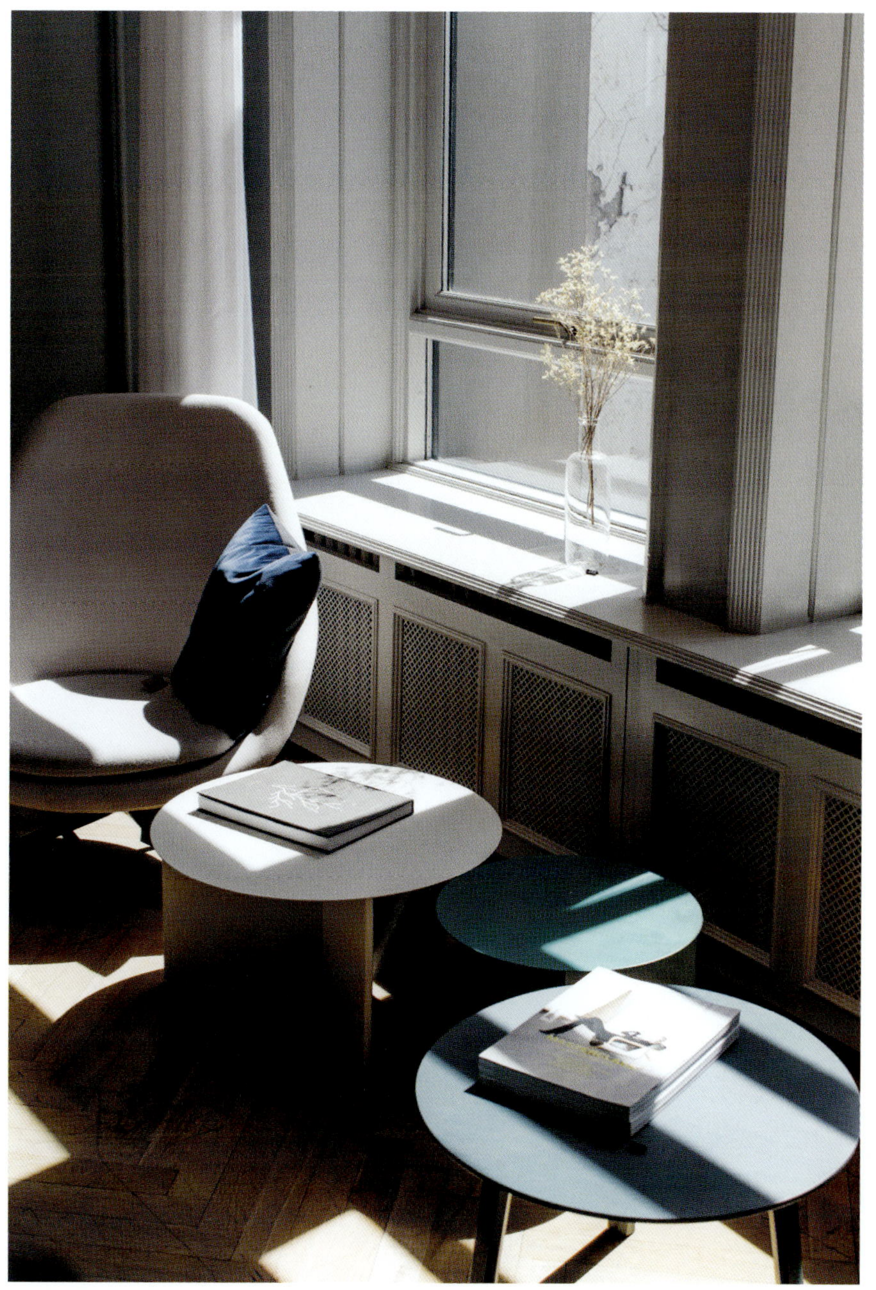

Saturday 10:10 AM

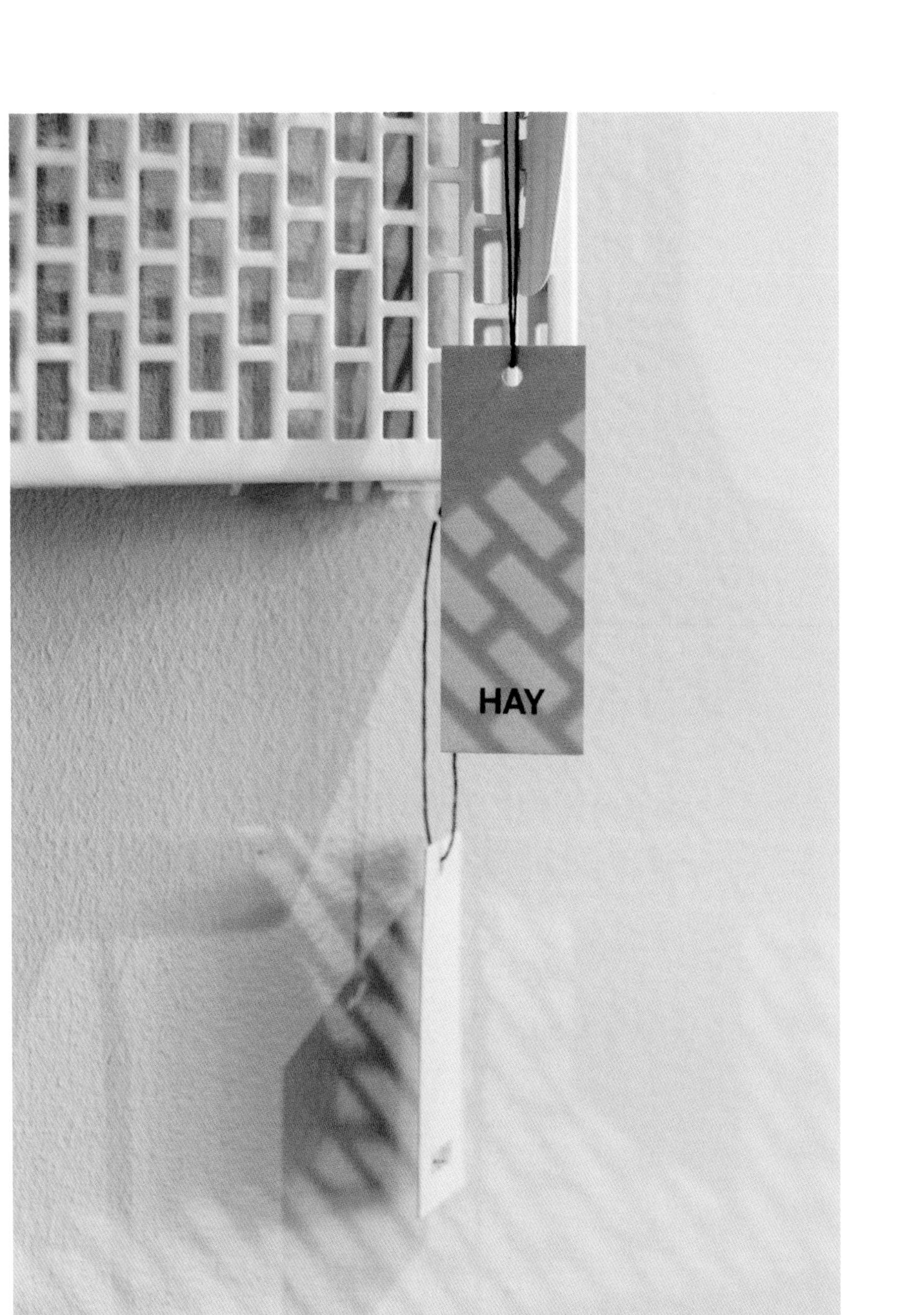
HAY

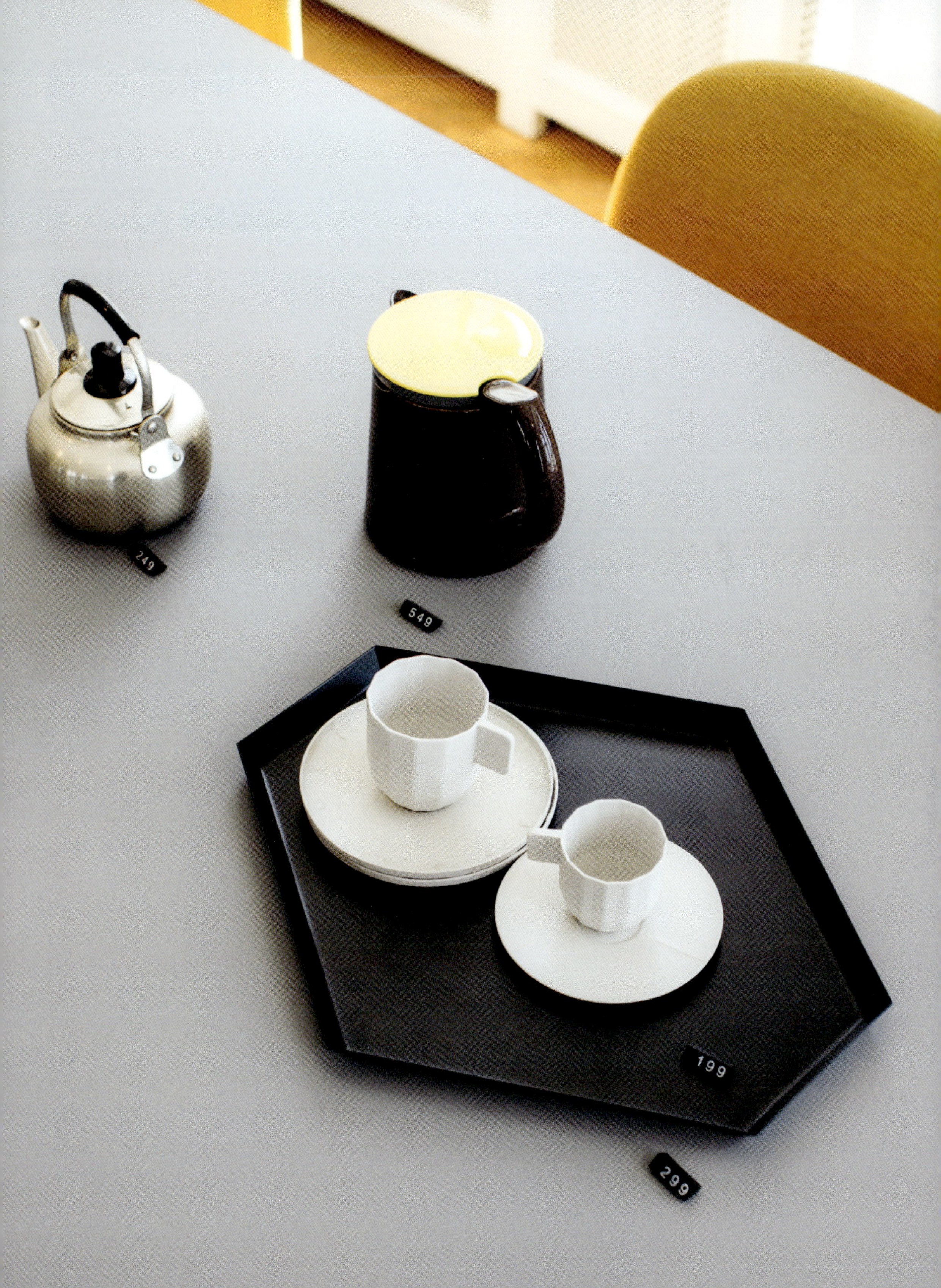
249
549
199
299

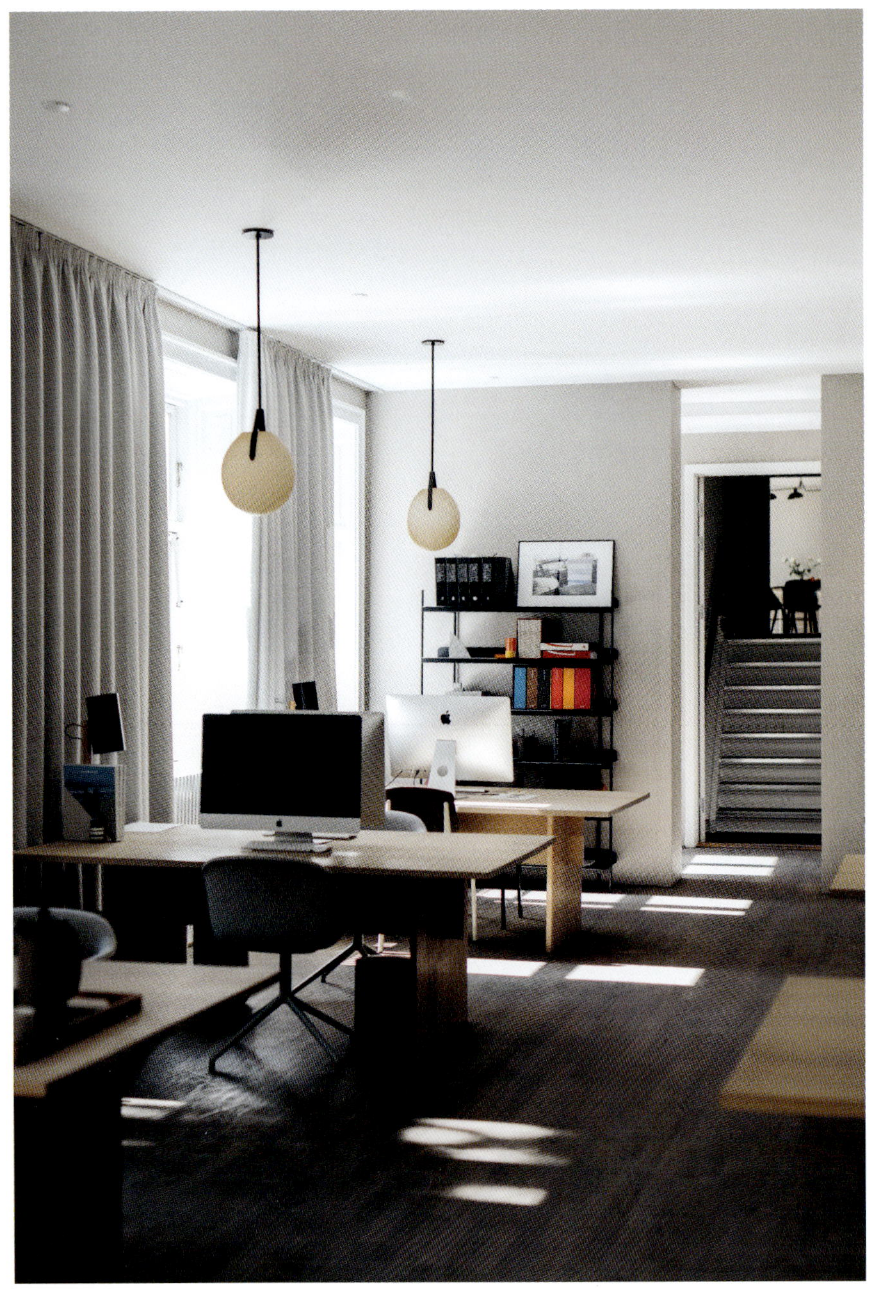

The Kinfolk Gallery

Saturday 12:24 PM

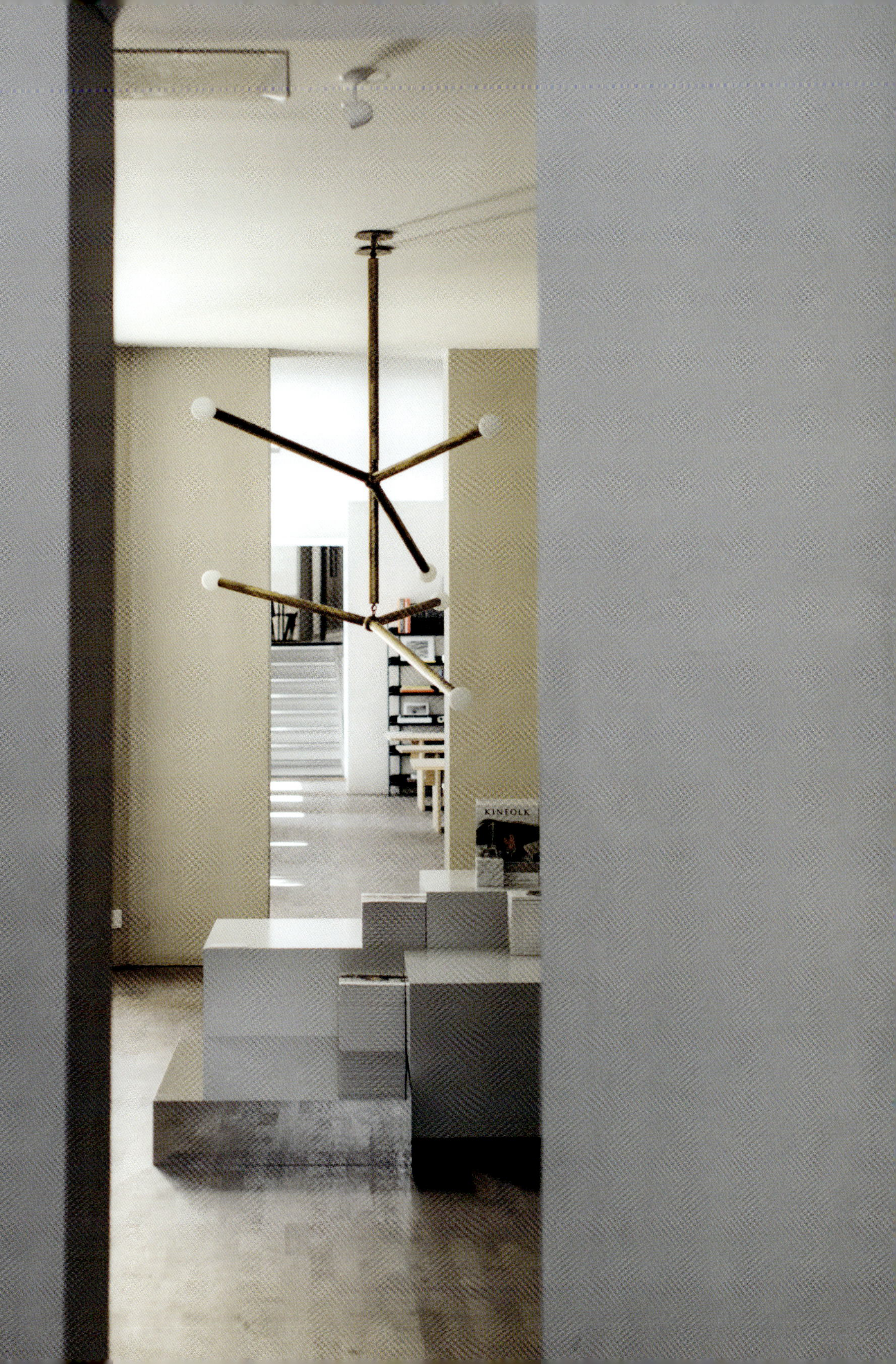
KINFOLK

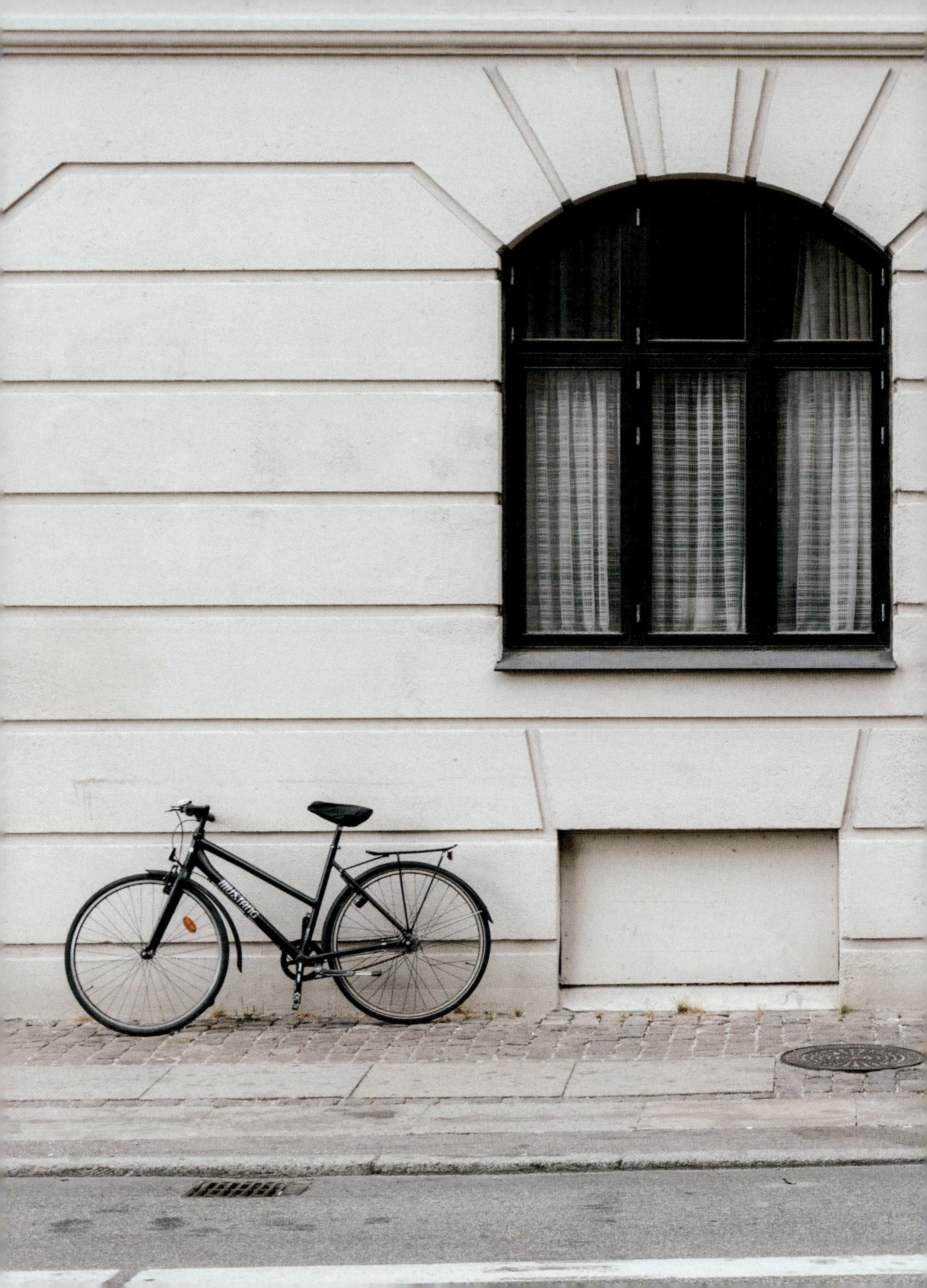
MUSTANG

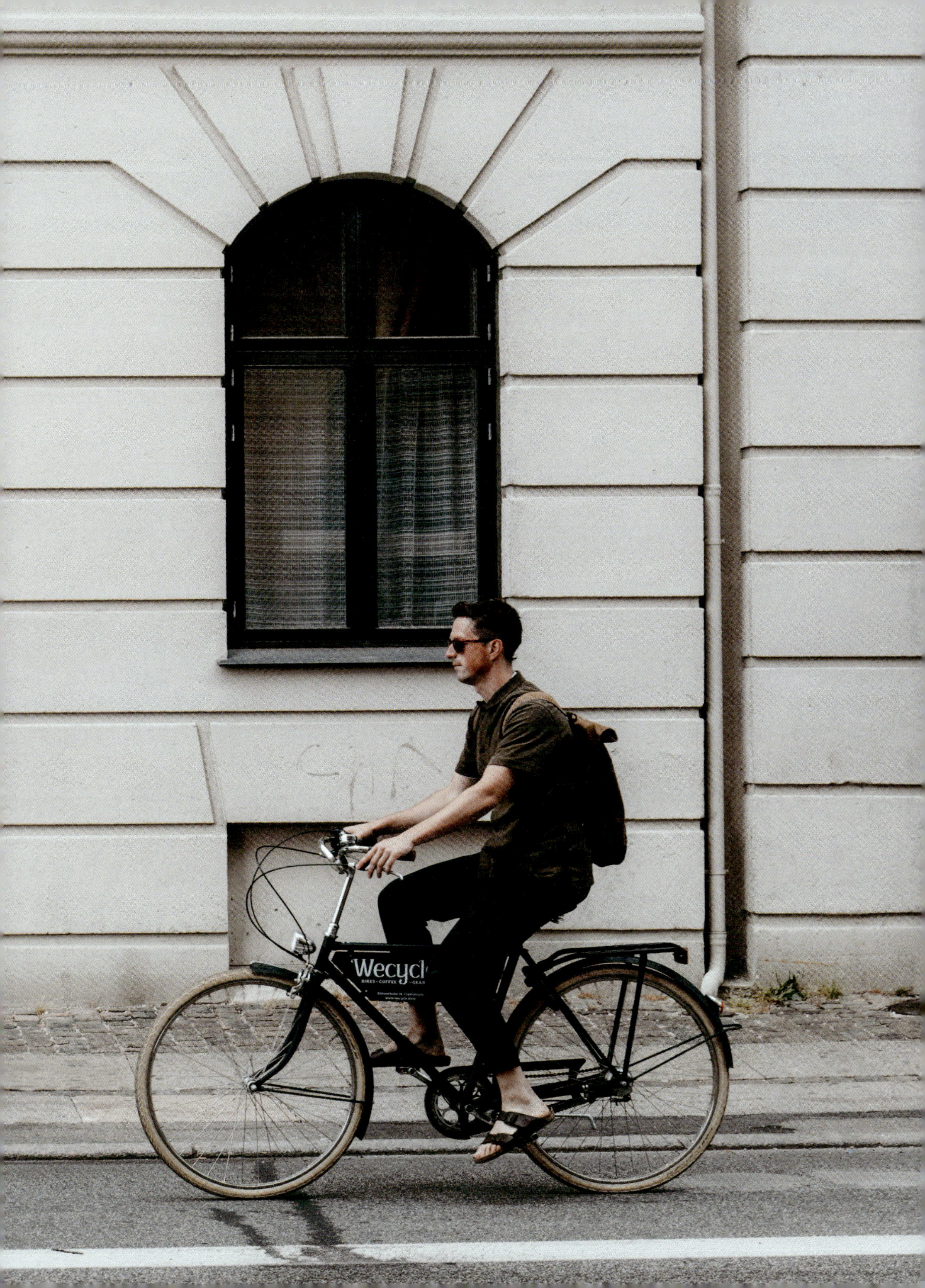
Wecycl
BIKES – COFFEE – GEAR

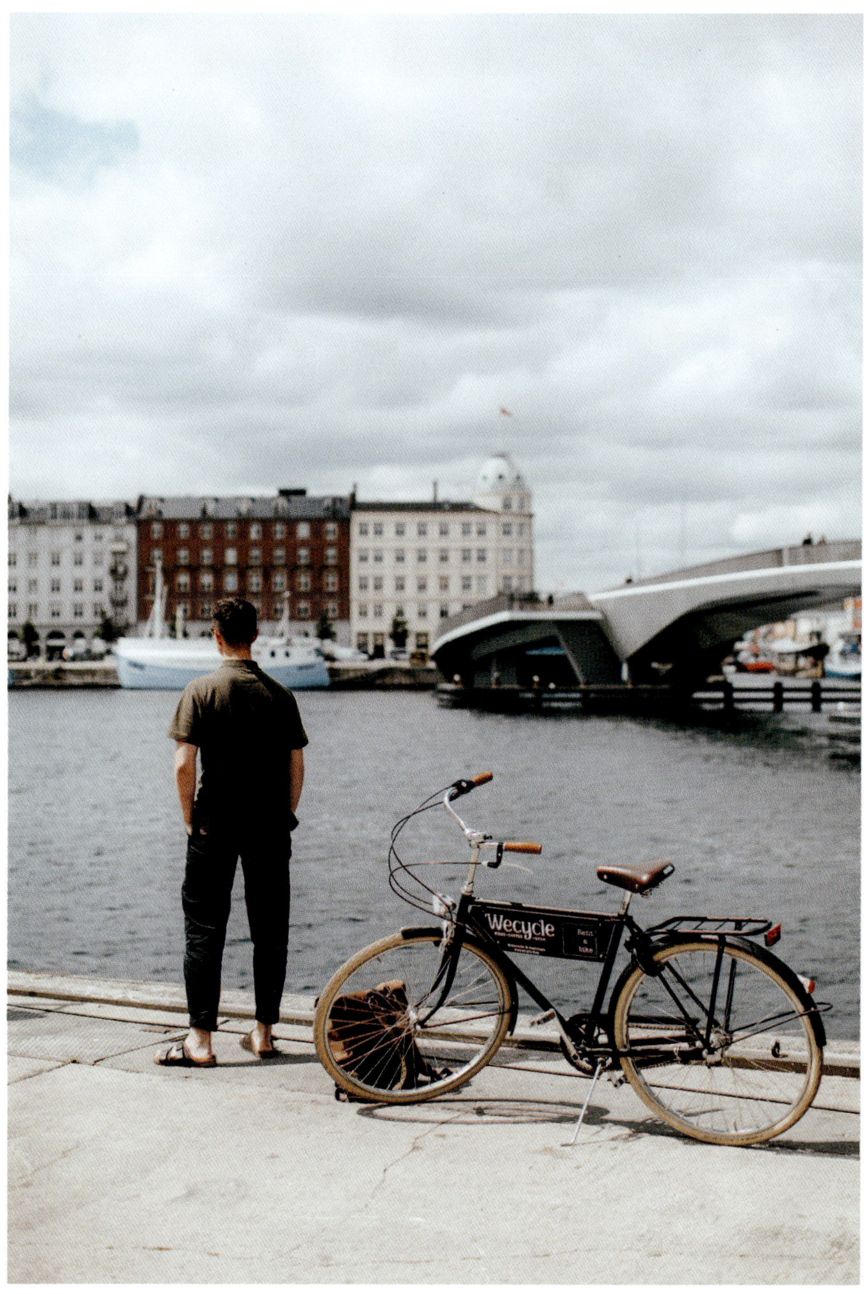

A city on the water

Saturday 2:29 PM

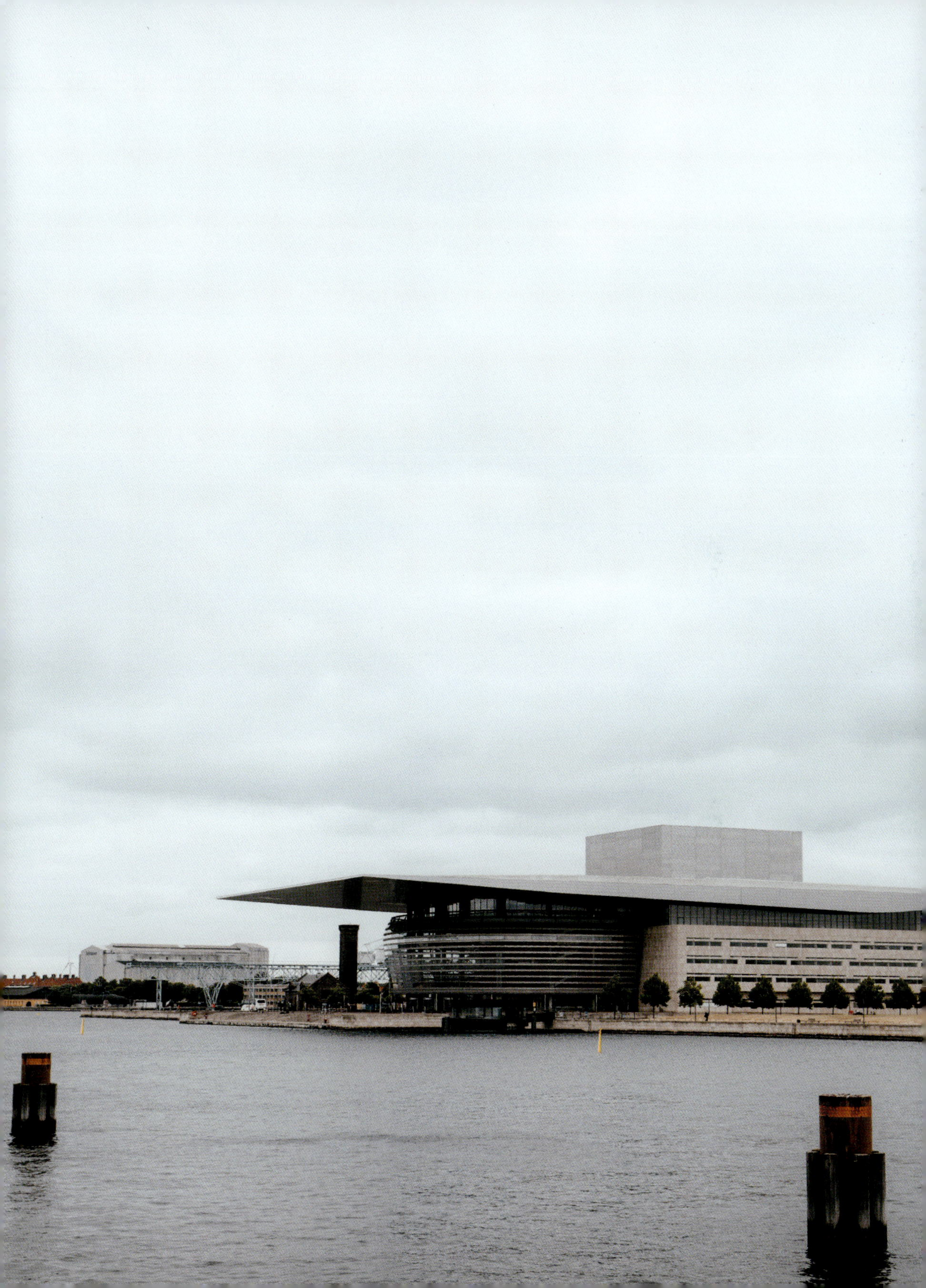

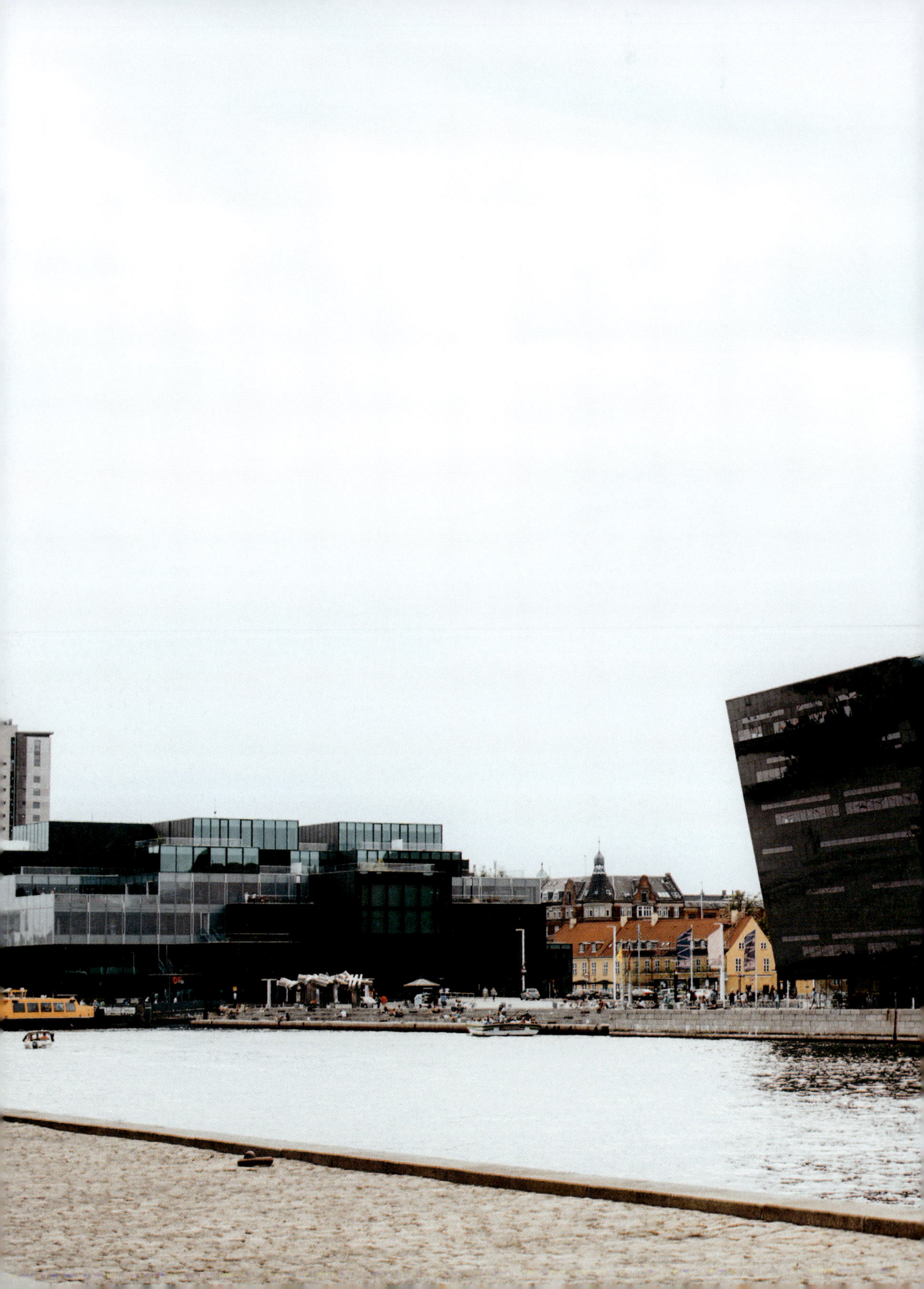

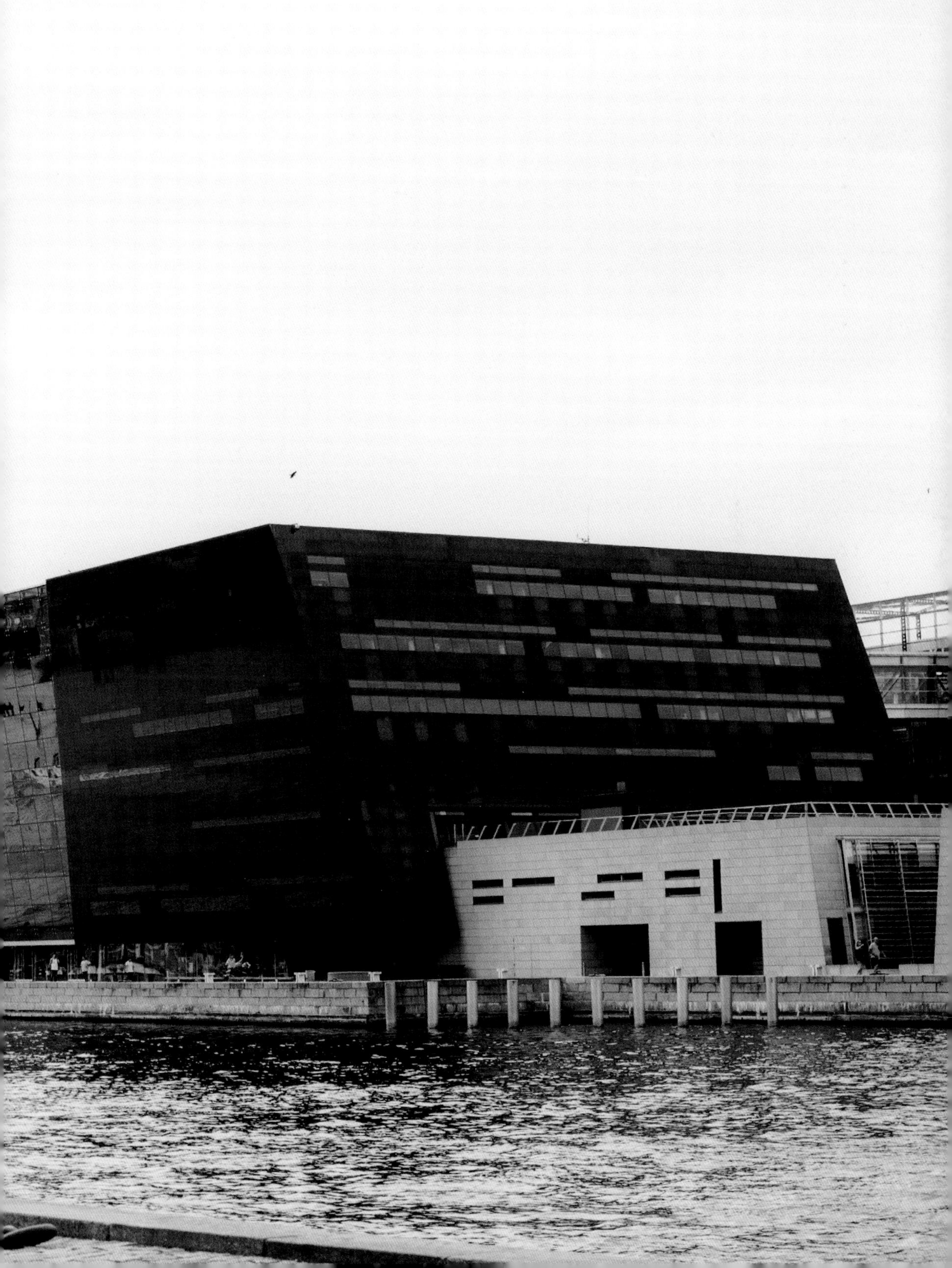

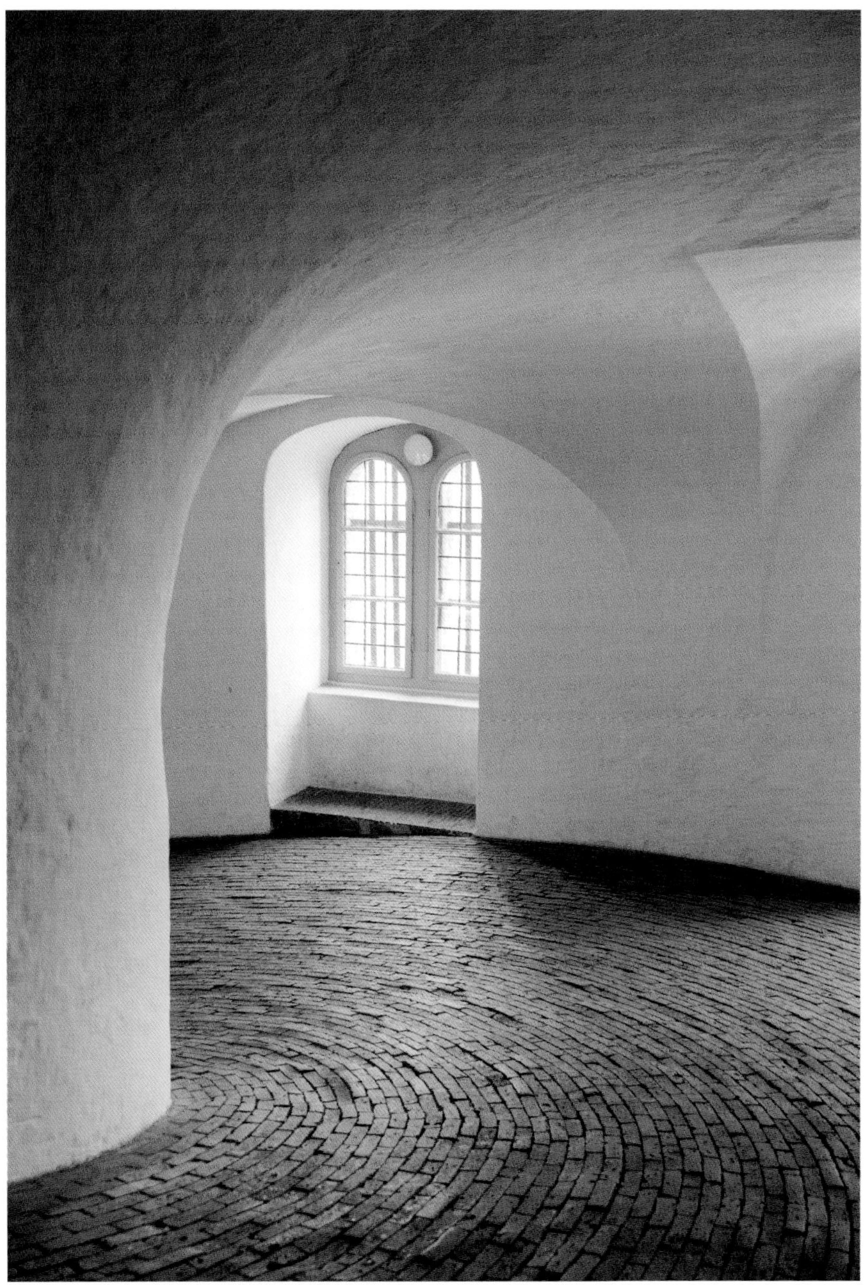

Rundetaarn

Saturday 4:21 PM

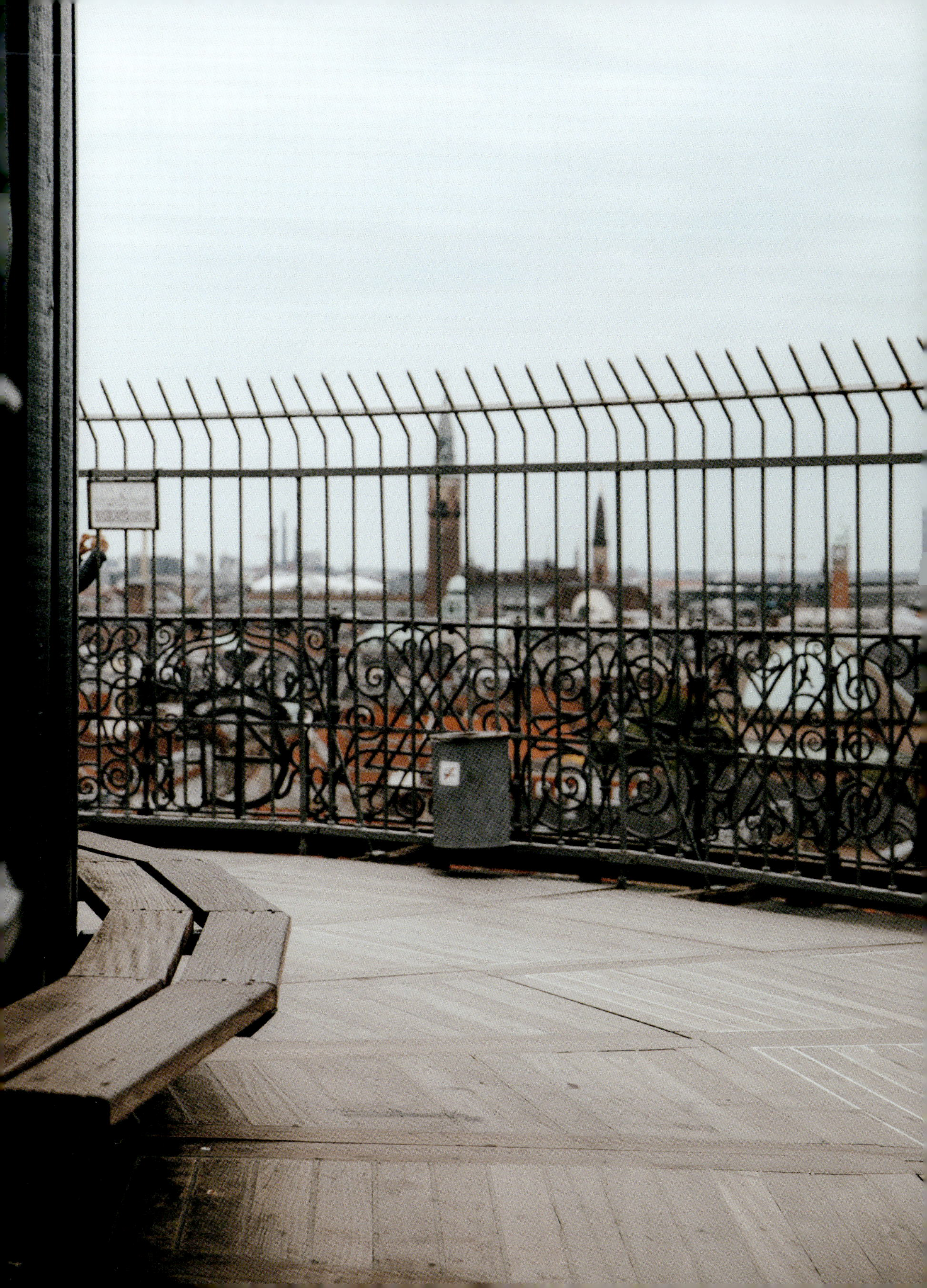

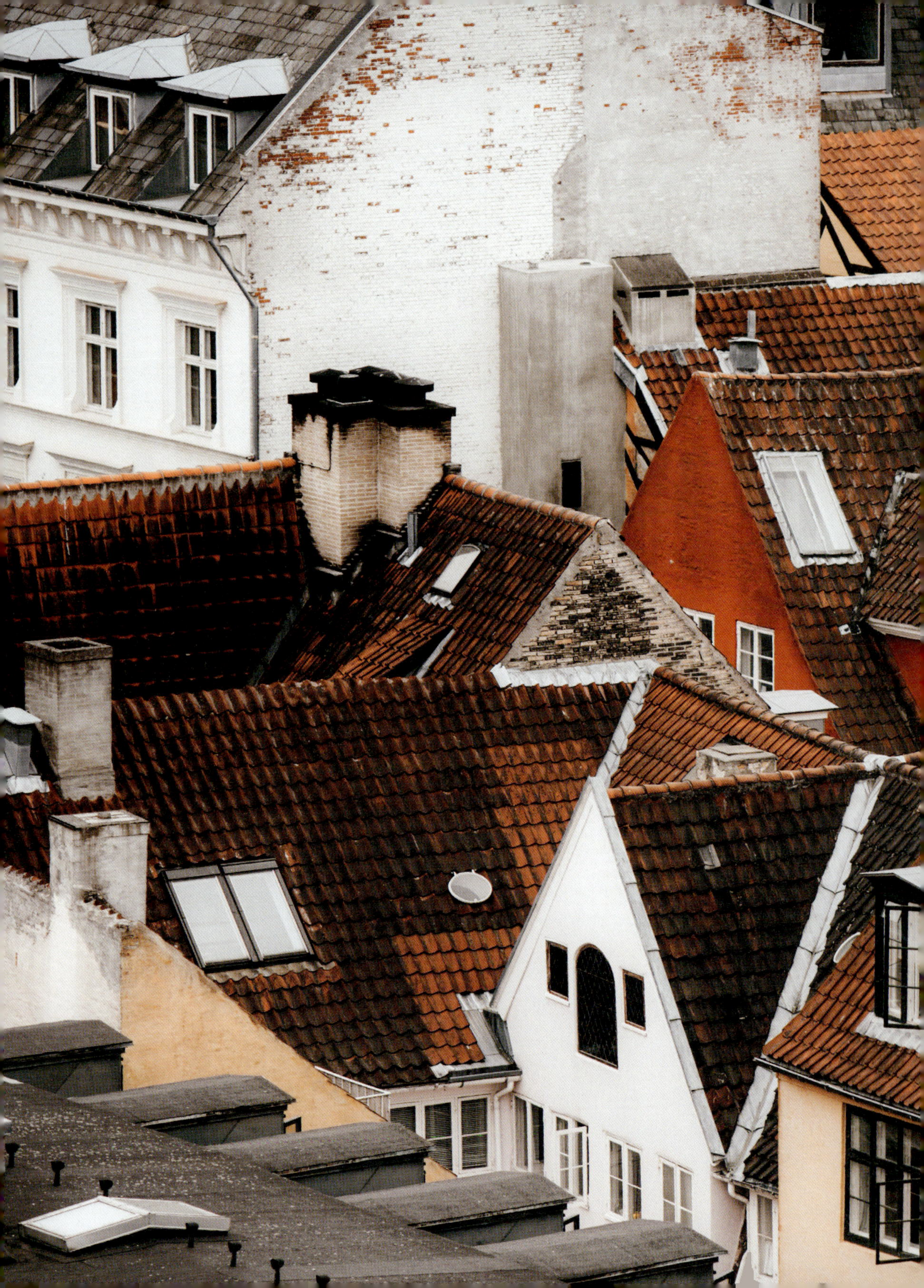

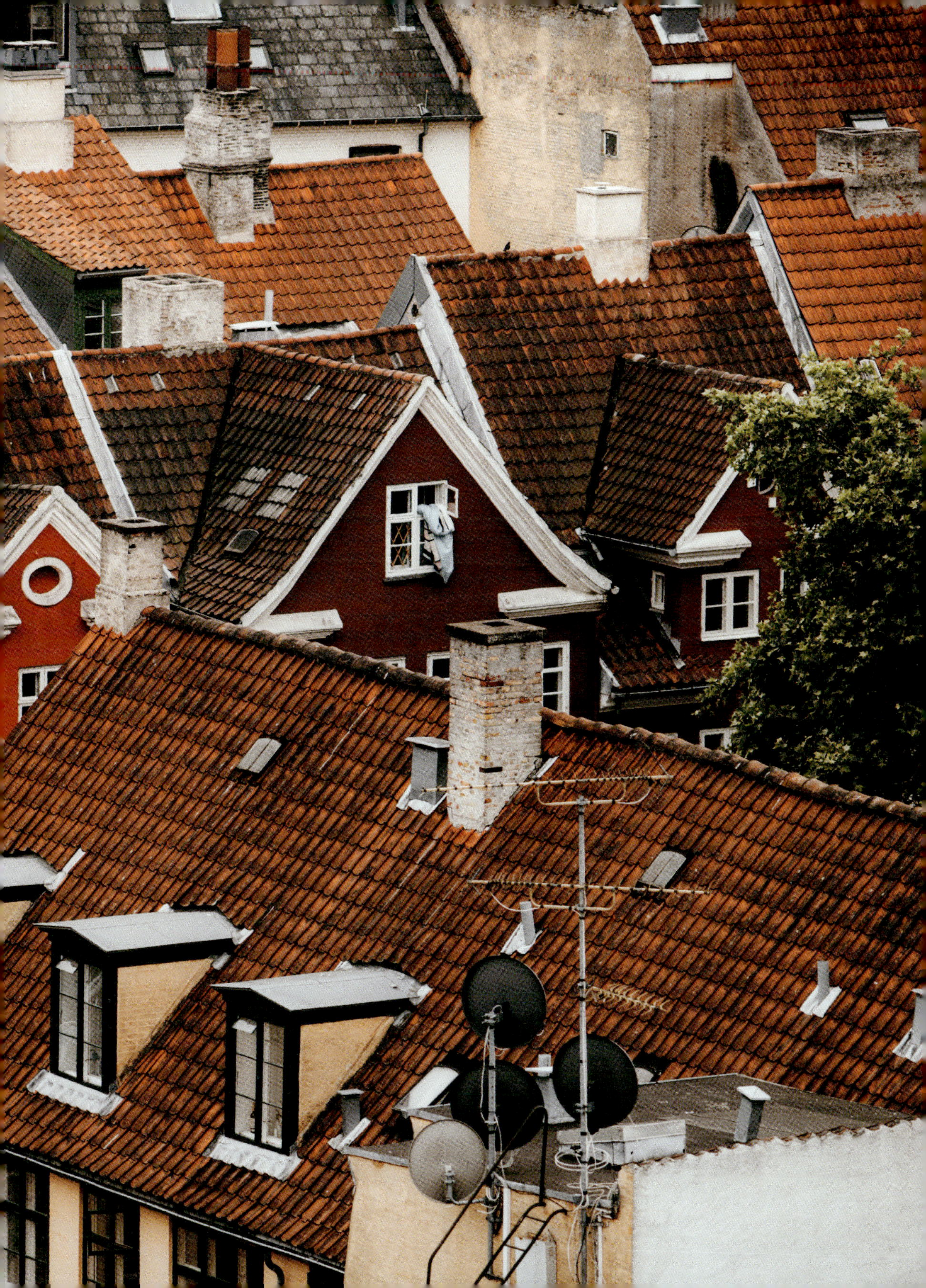

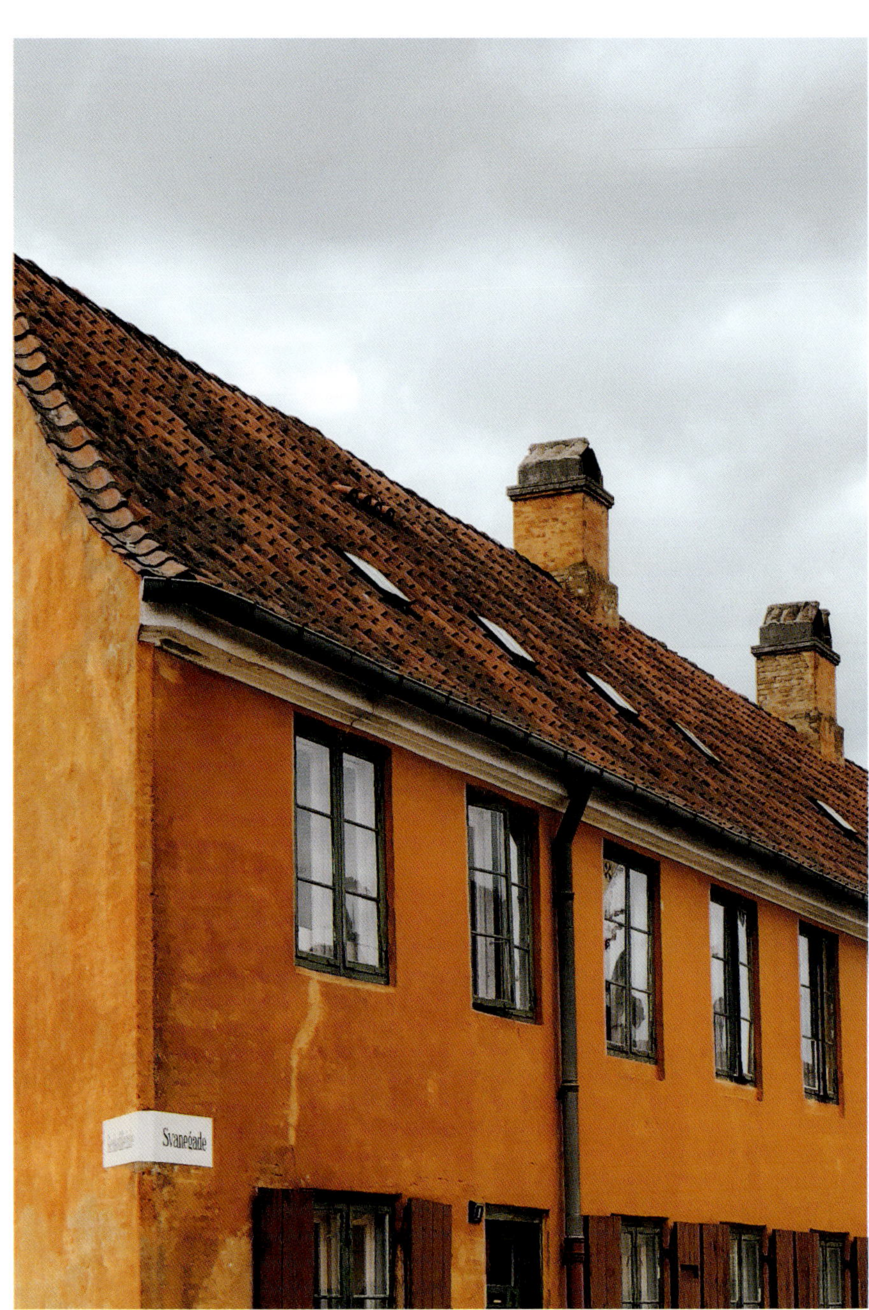
Svanegade

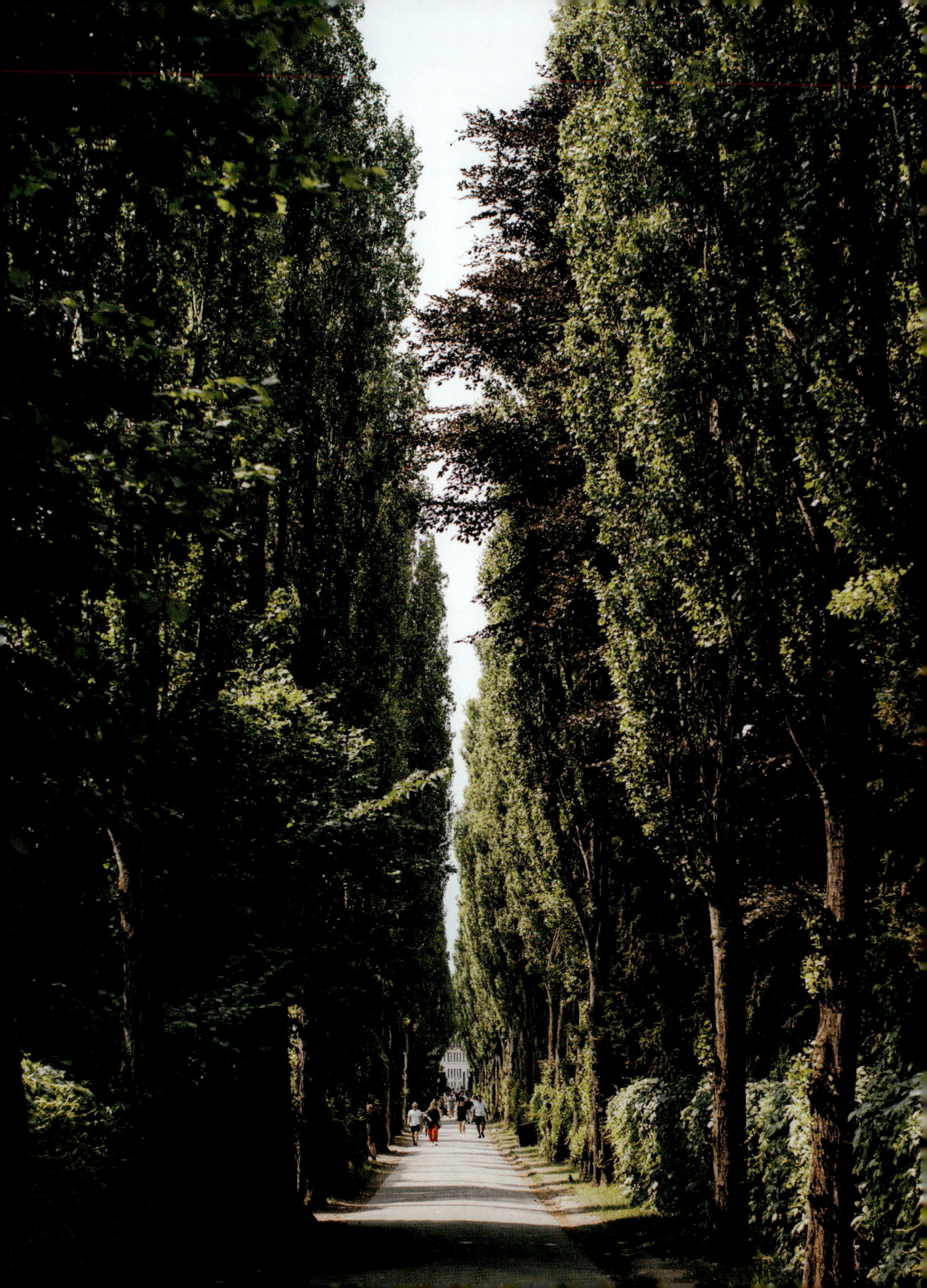

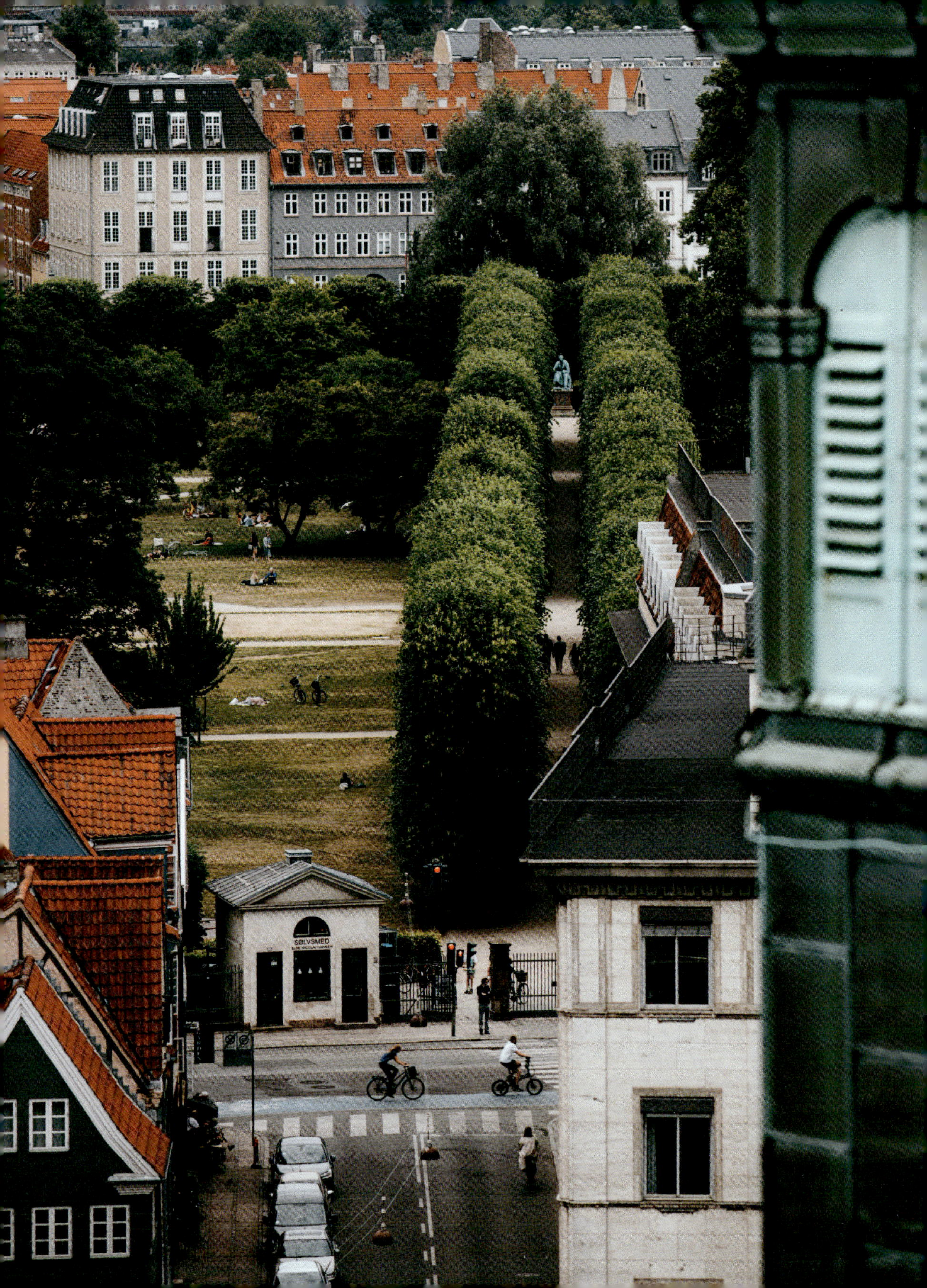
SØLVSMED

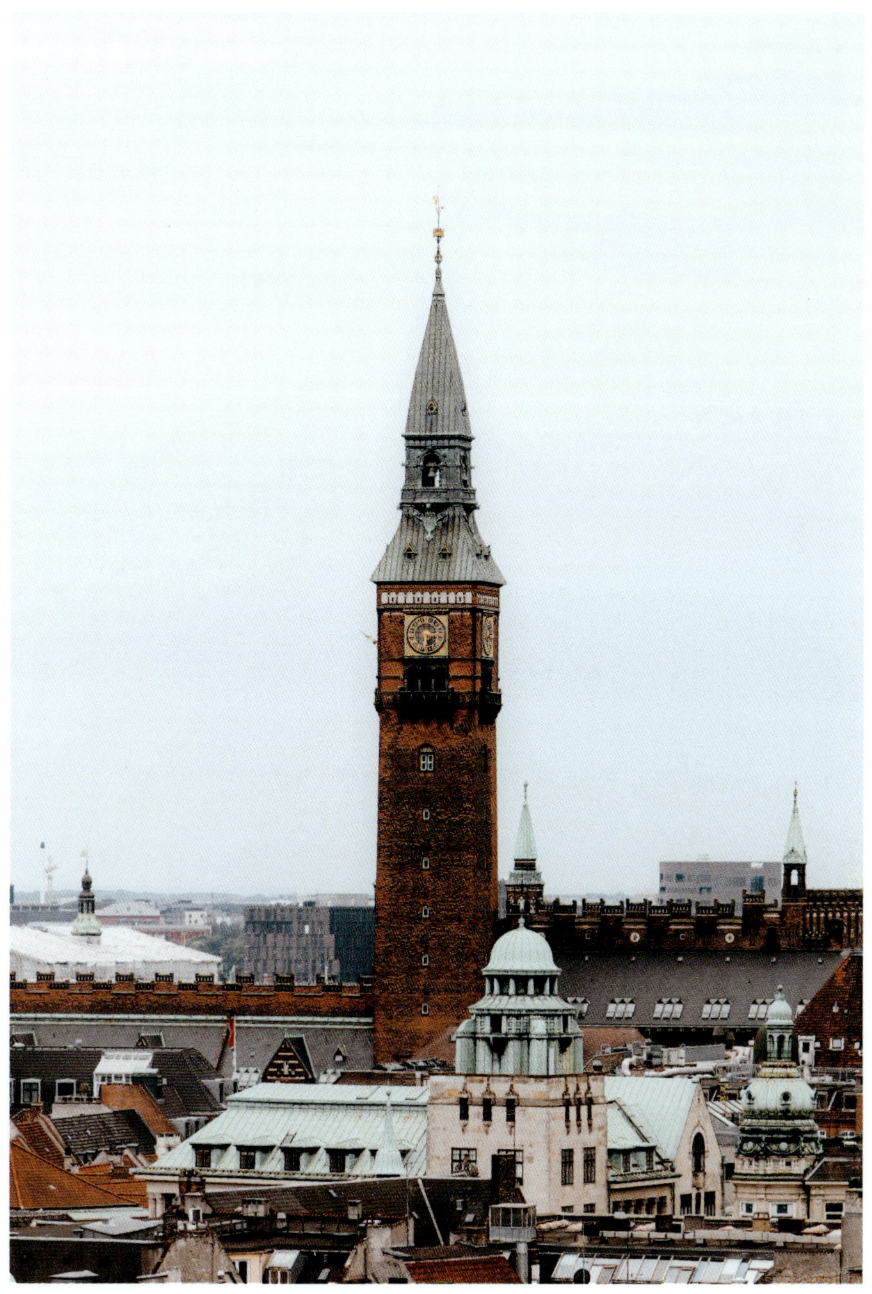

Saturday 4:37 PM

City views and rising spires

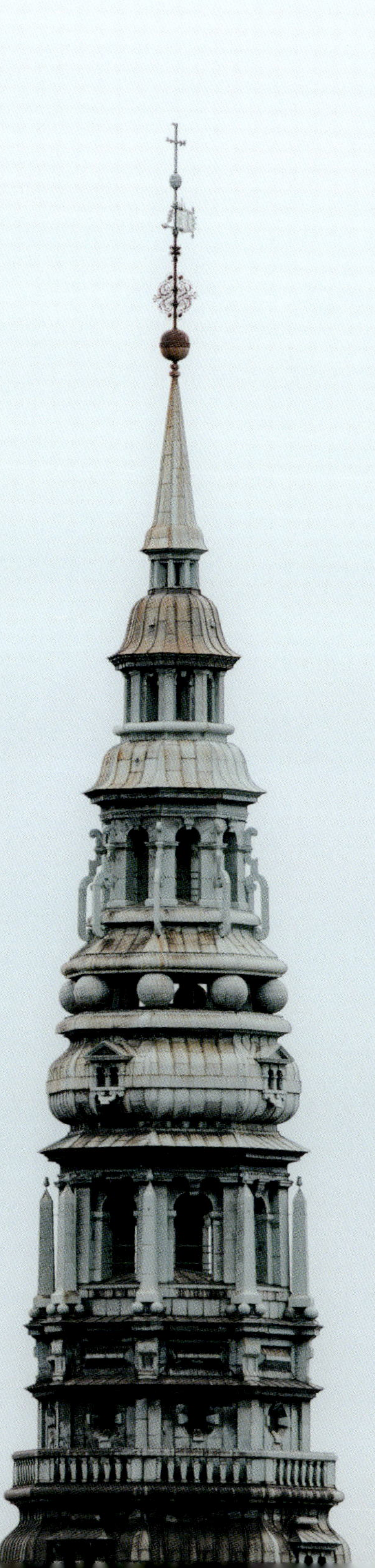

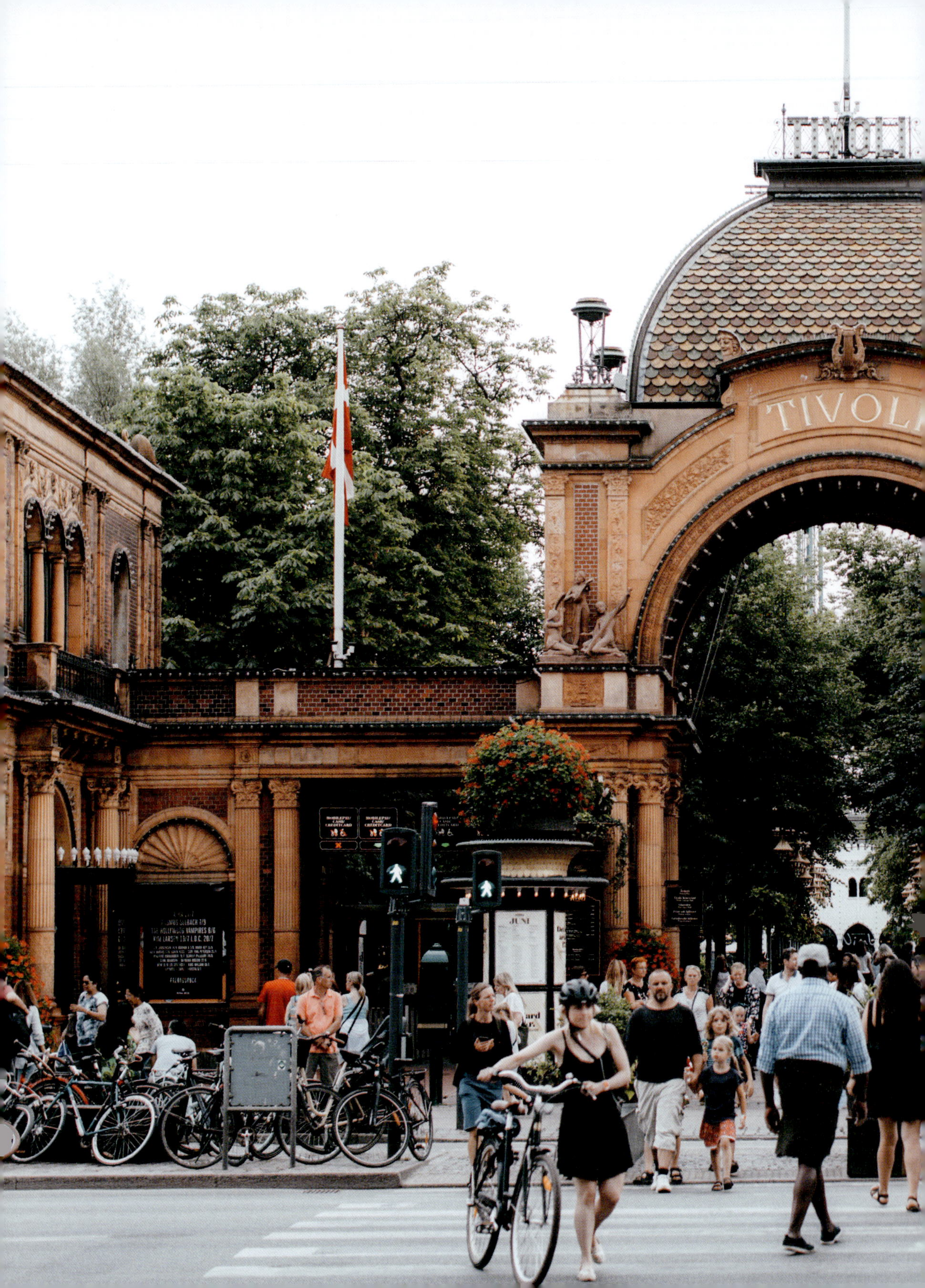
TIVOLI
TIVOLI
JUNI

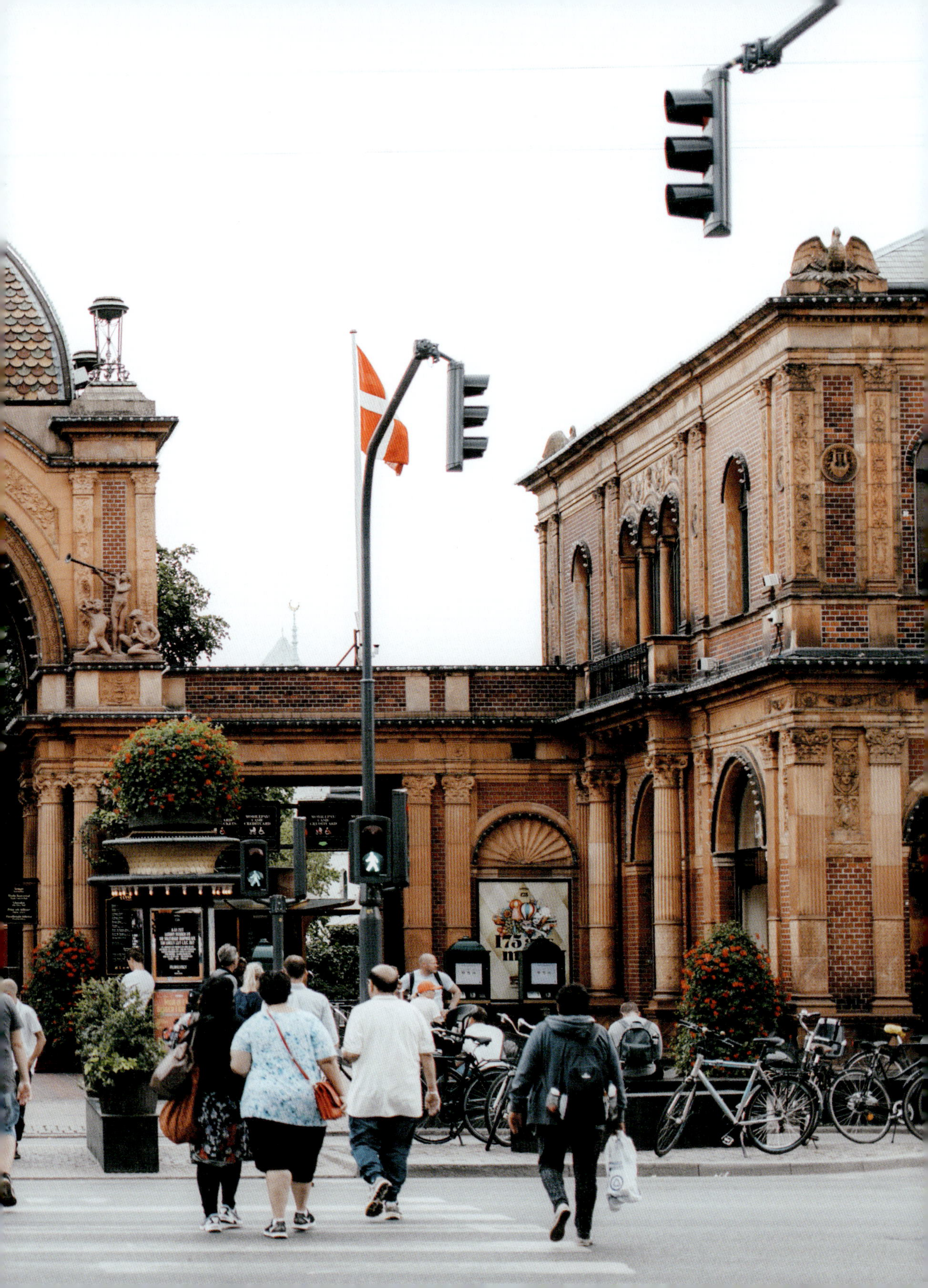

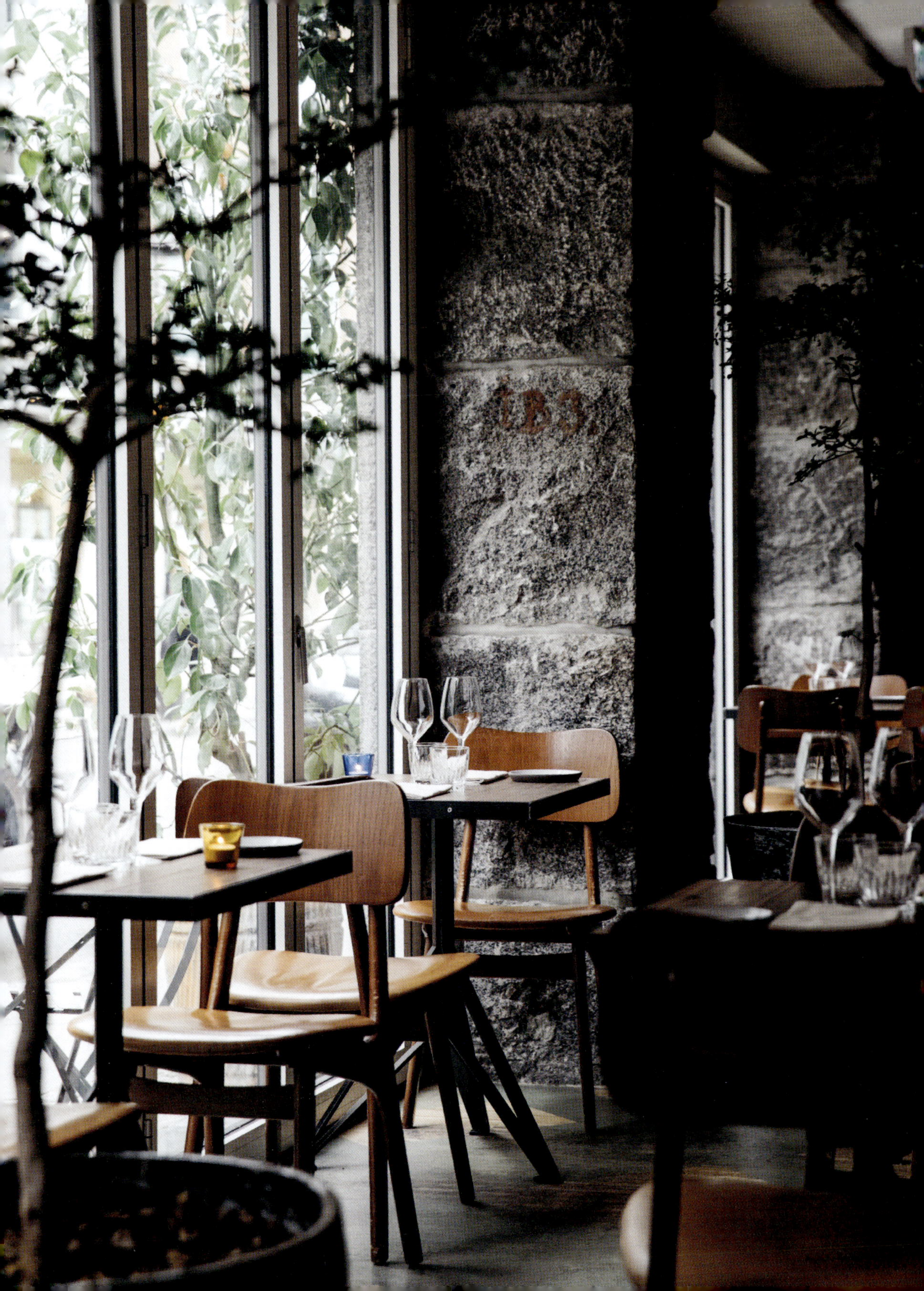

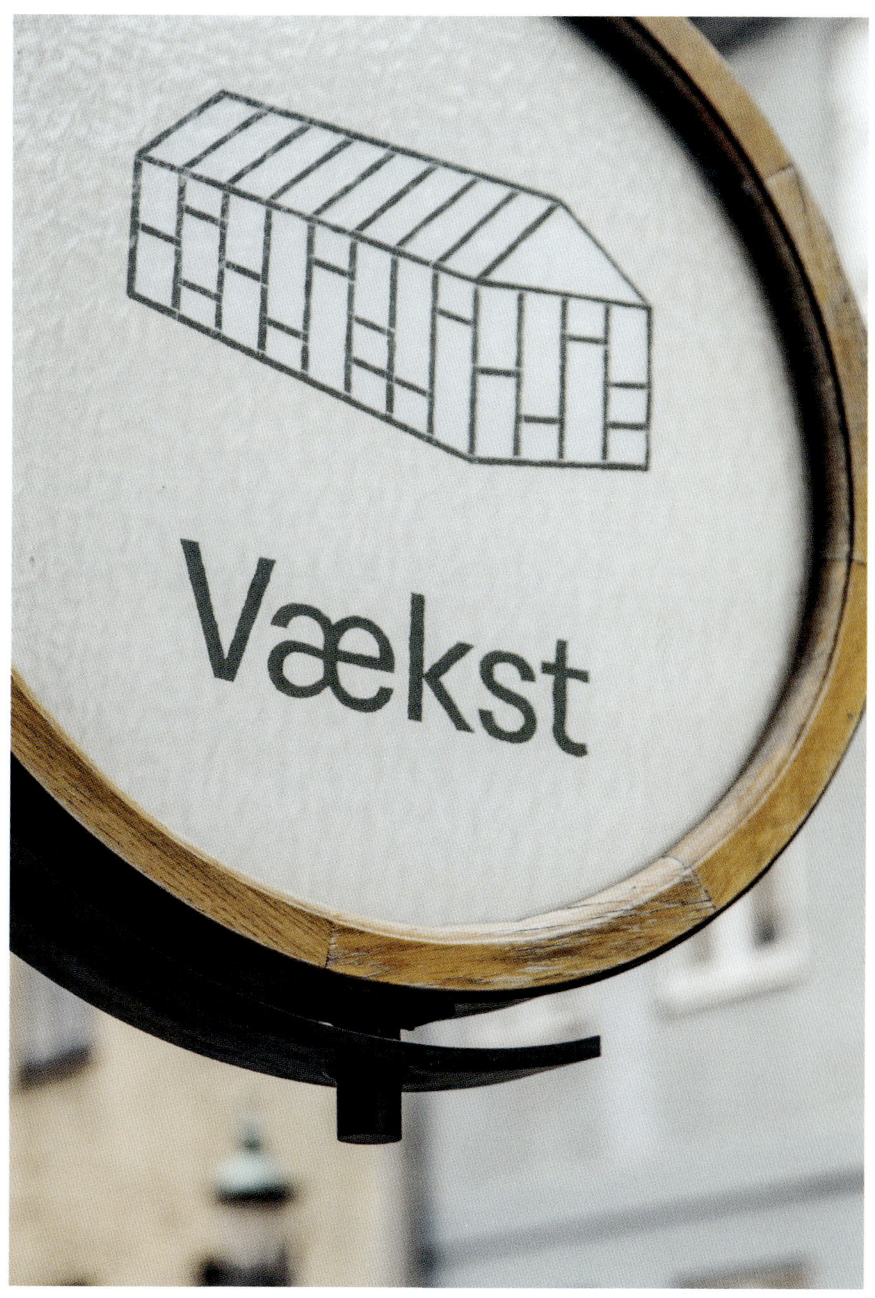

Saturday 8:00 PM

An evening meal of Nordic cuisine

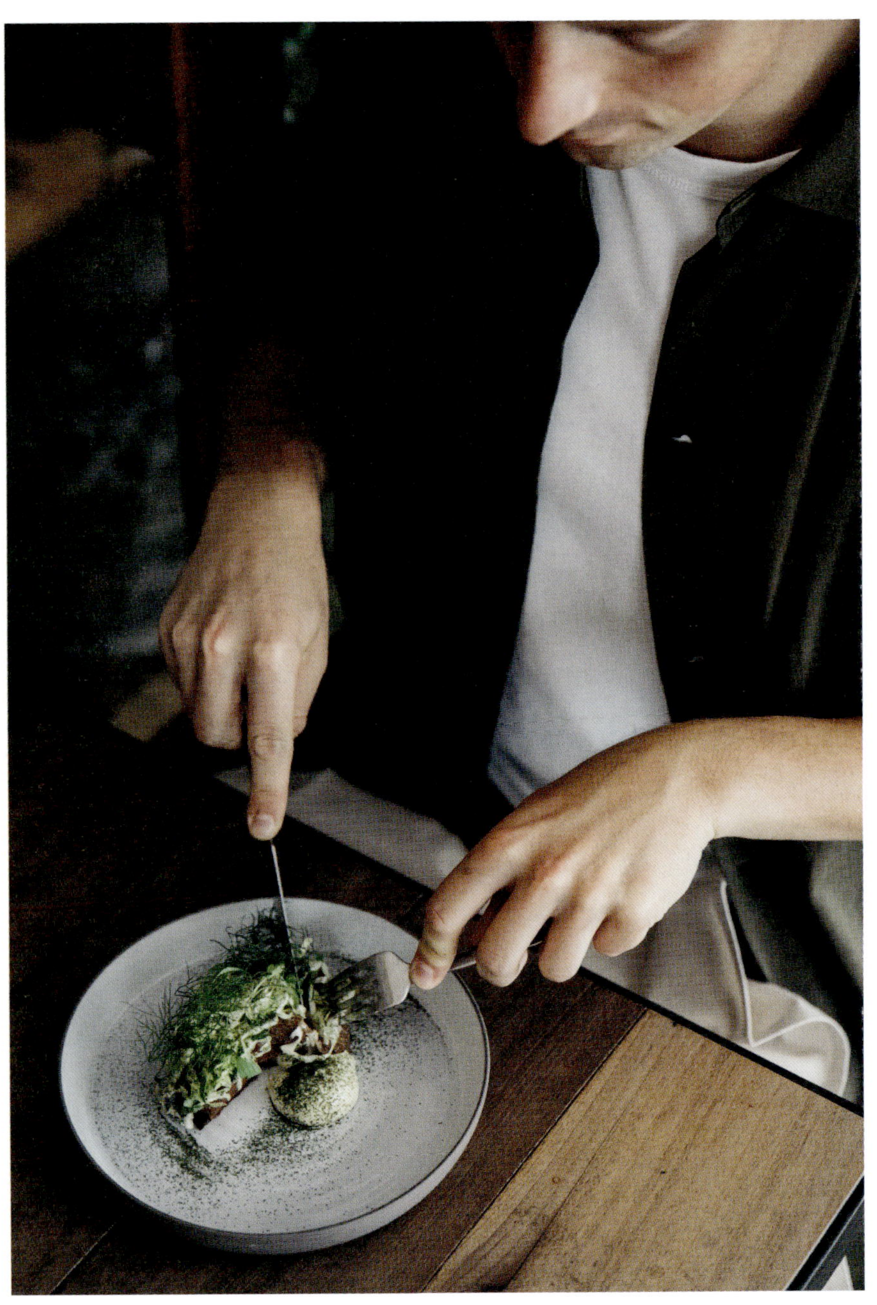

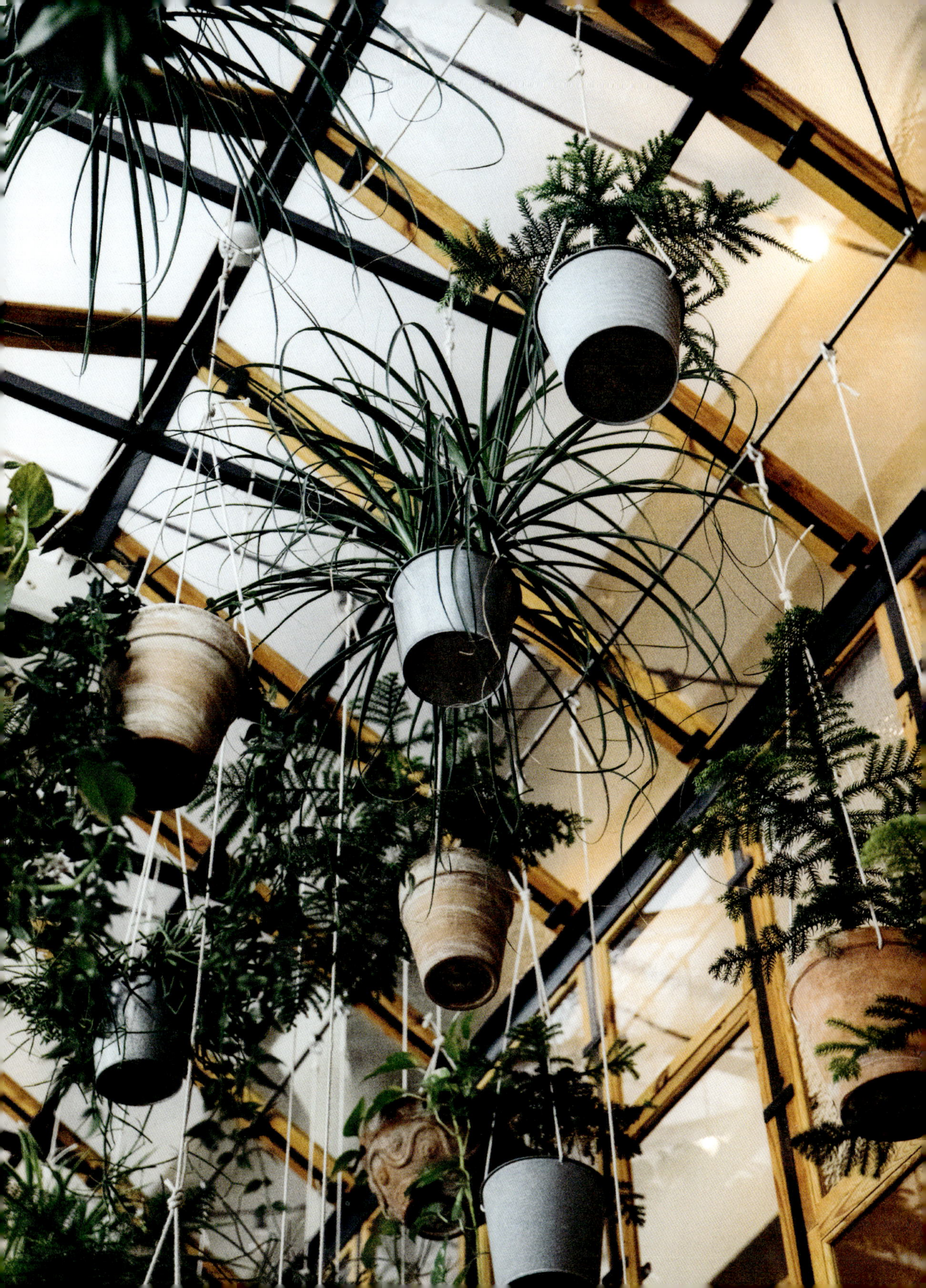

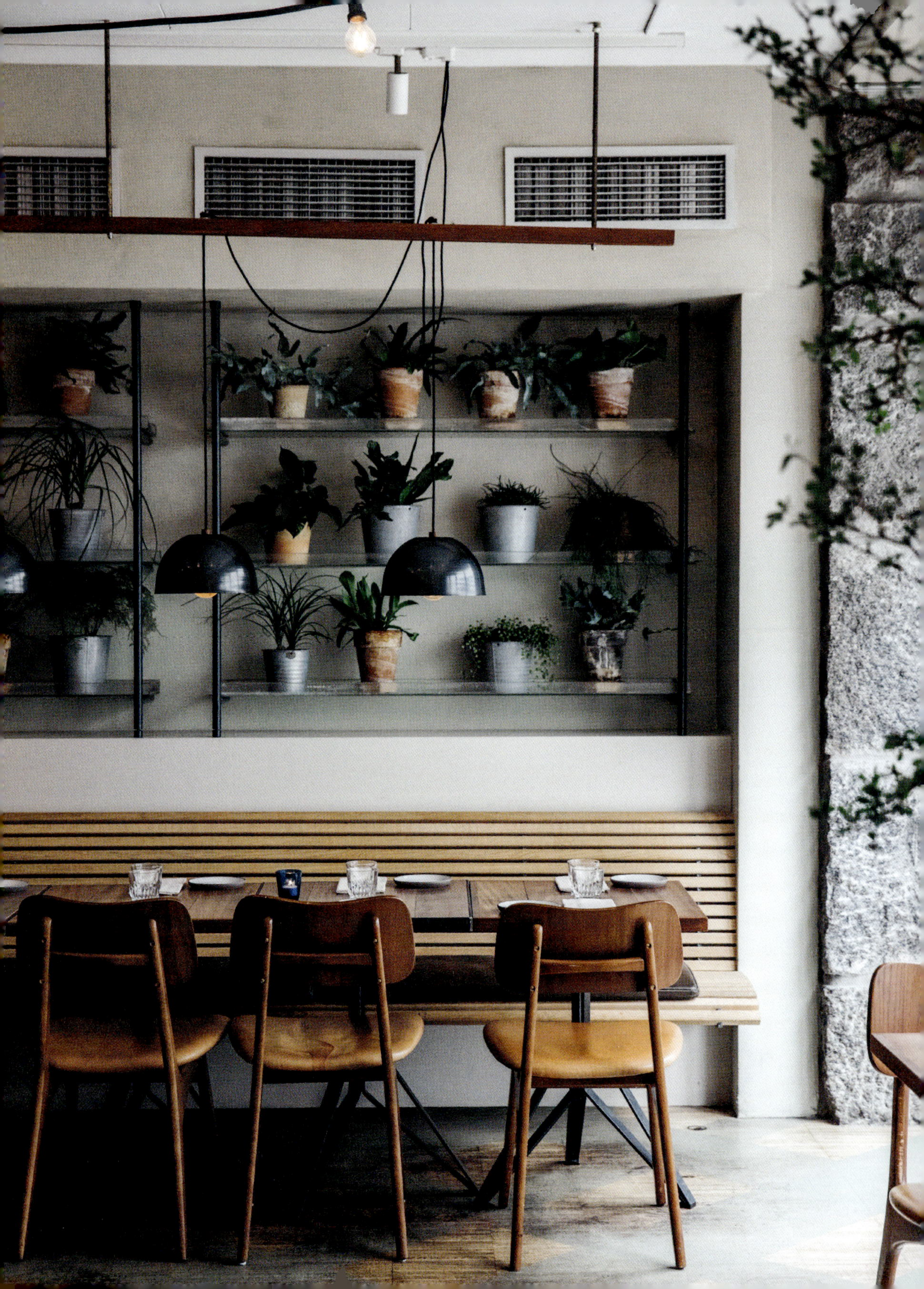

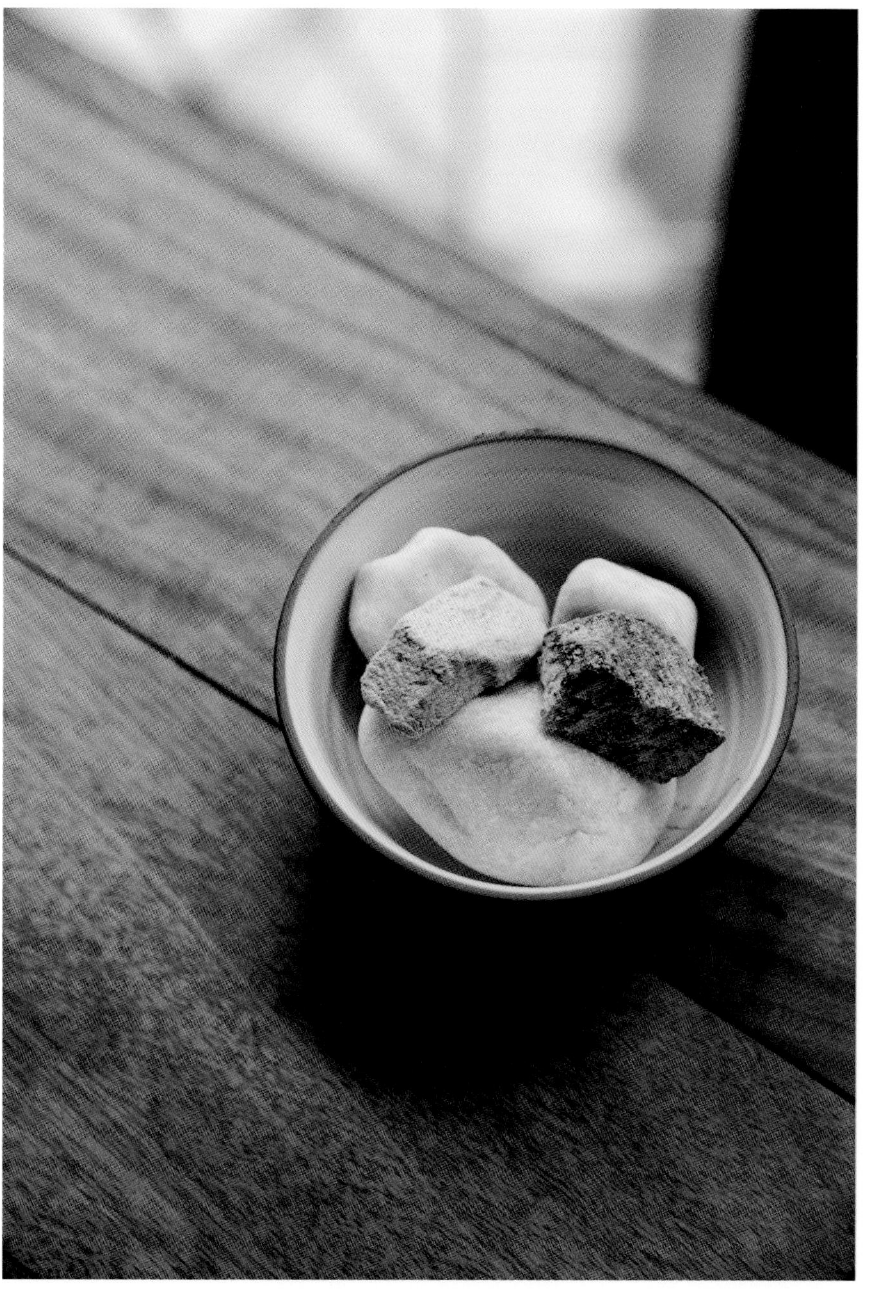

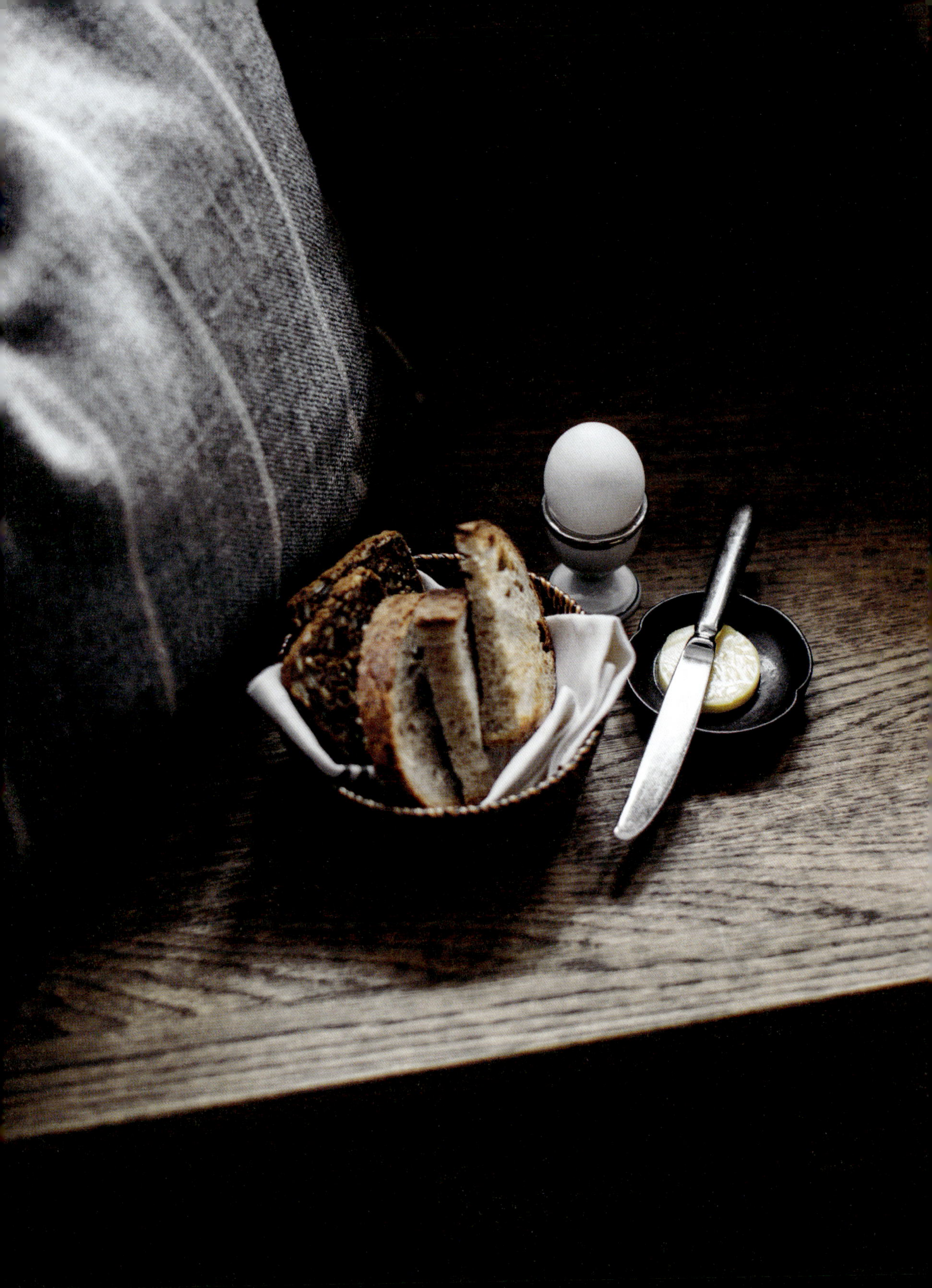

Sunday

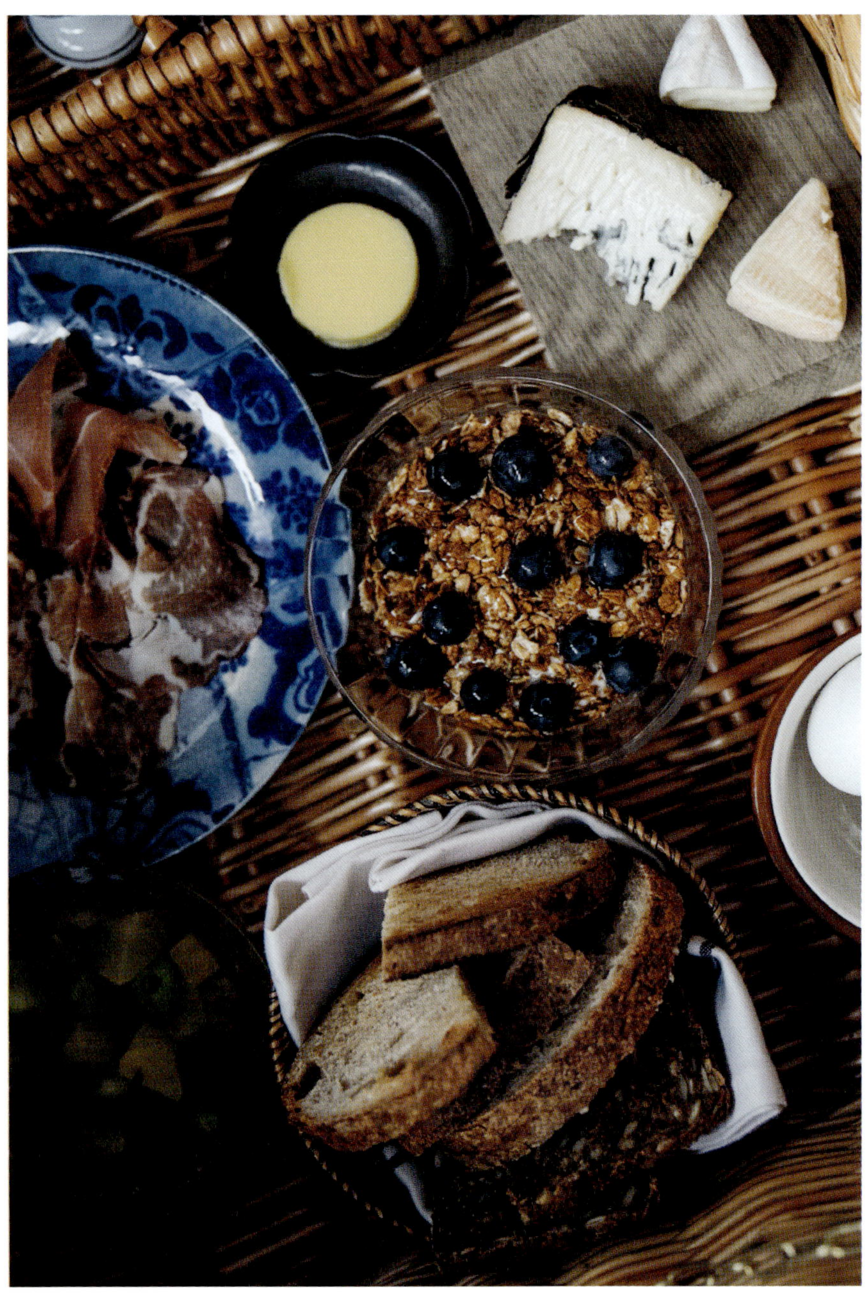

Breakfast at Hotel Sanders

Sunday 9:15 AM

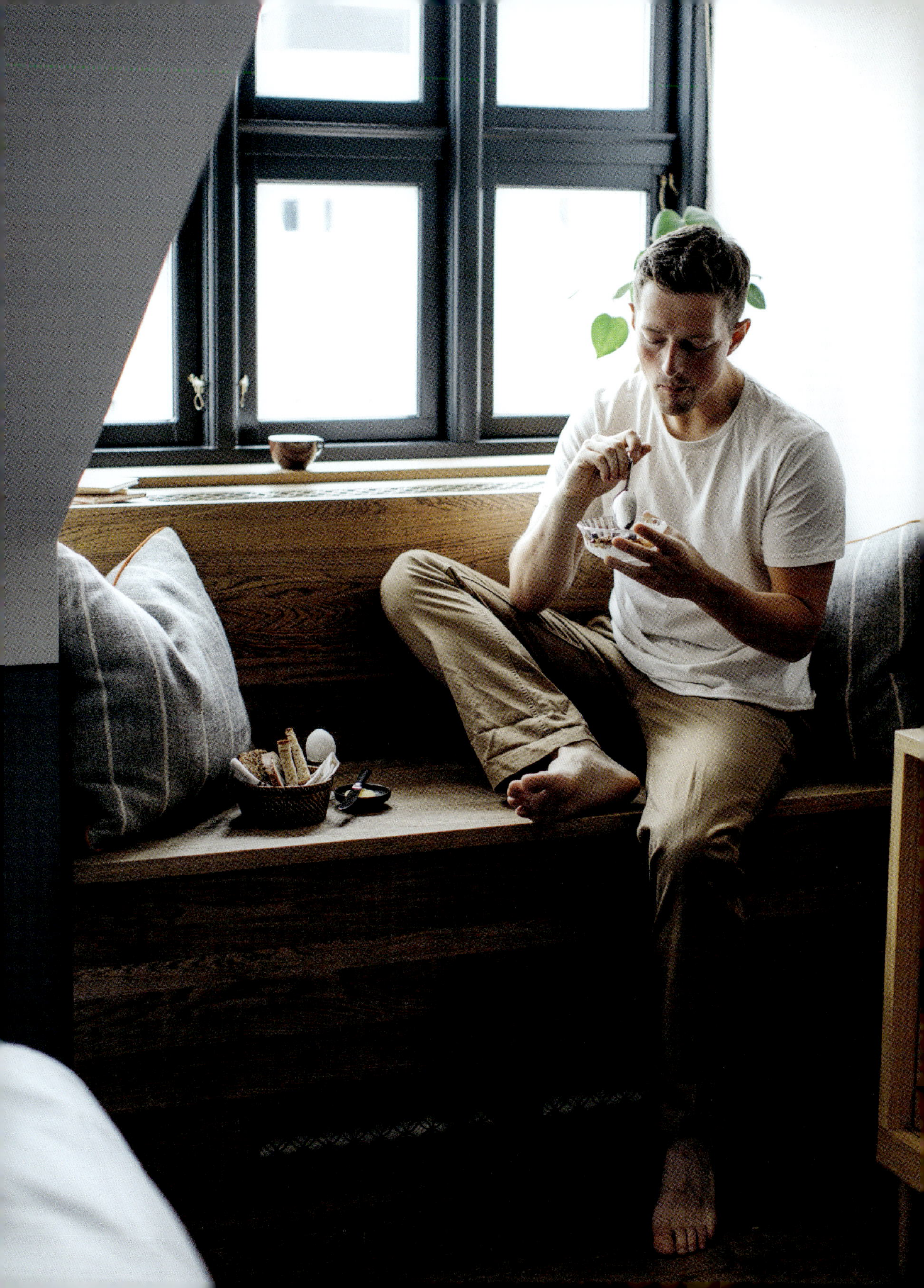

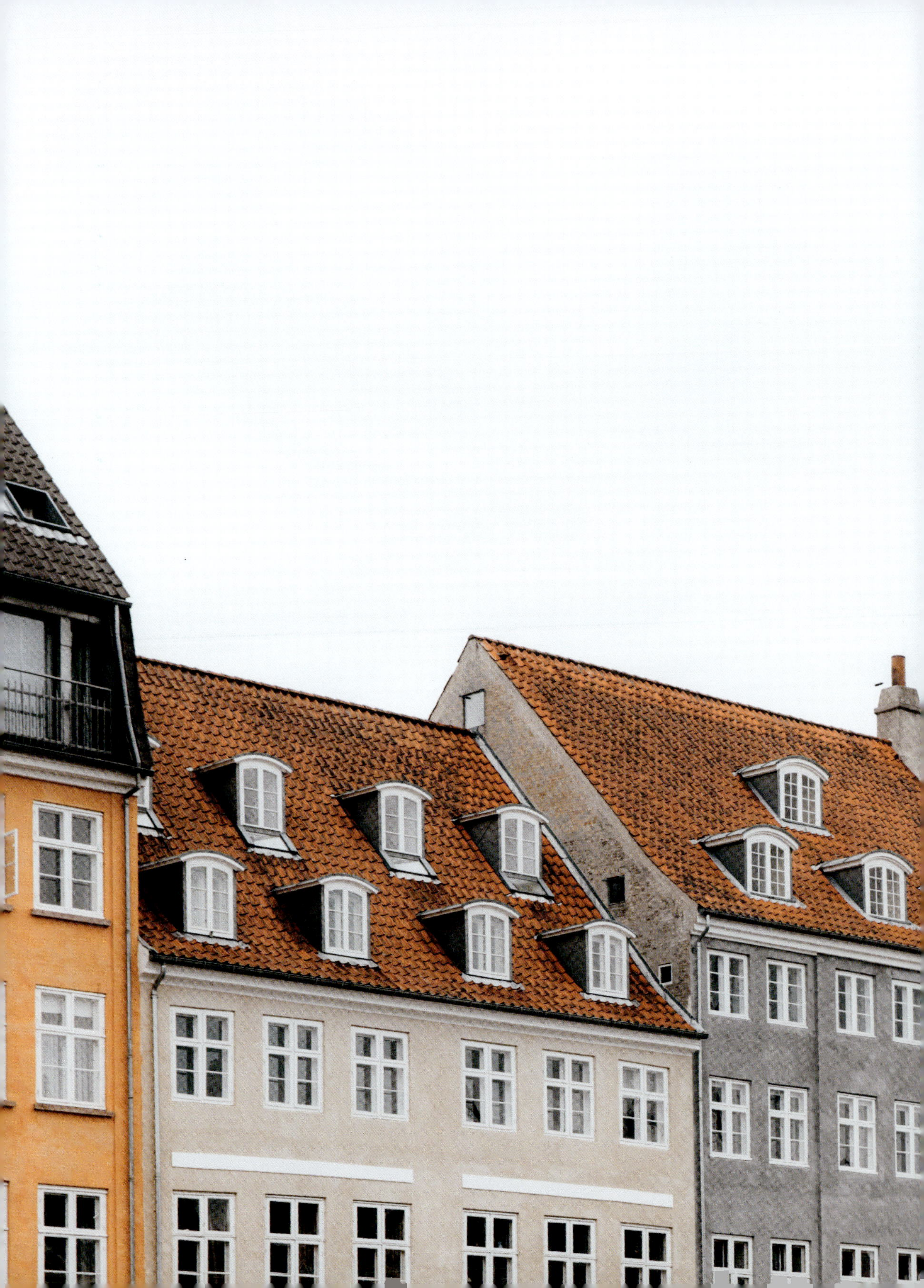

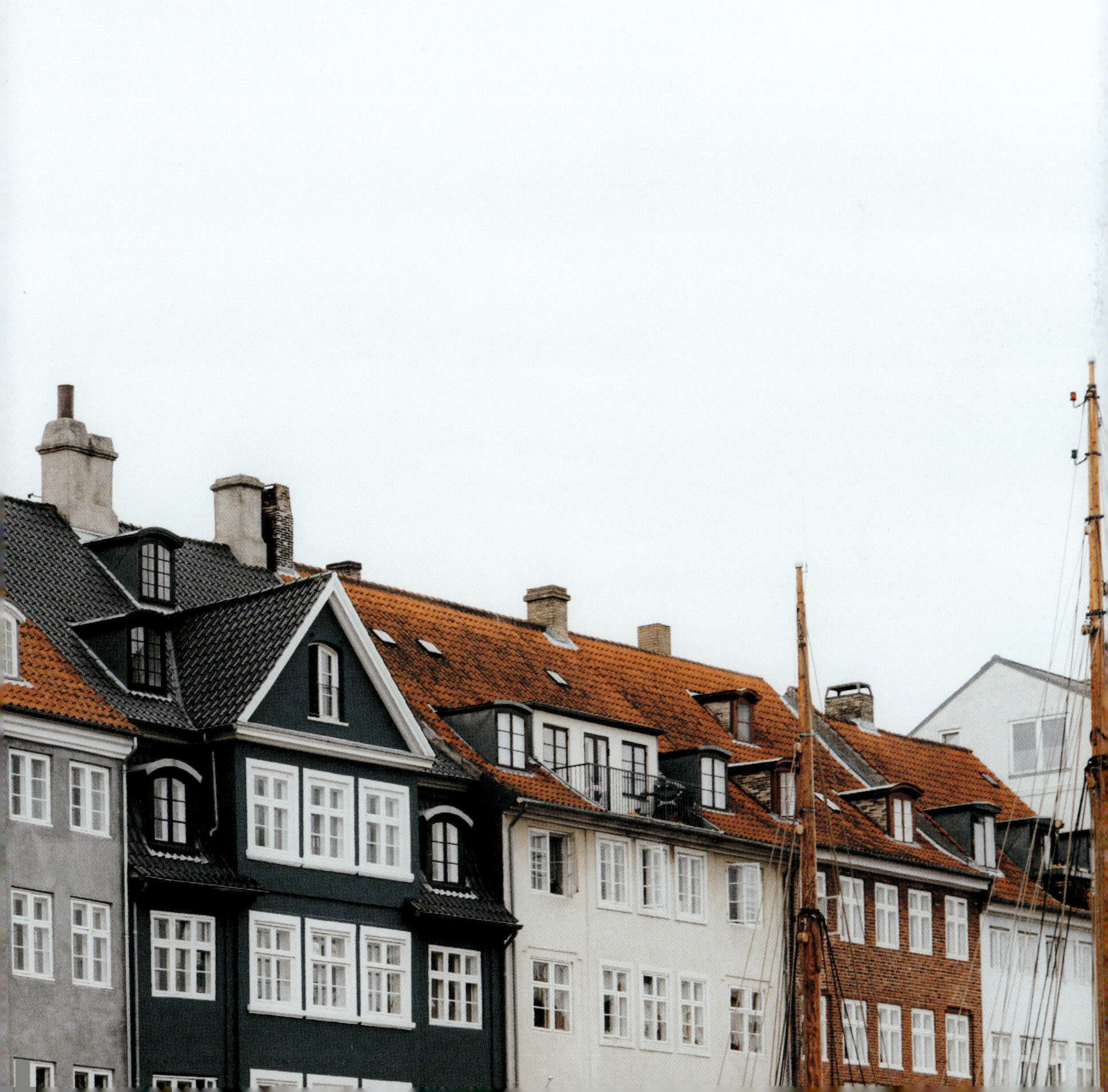

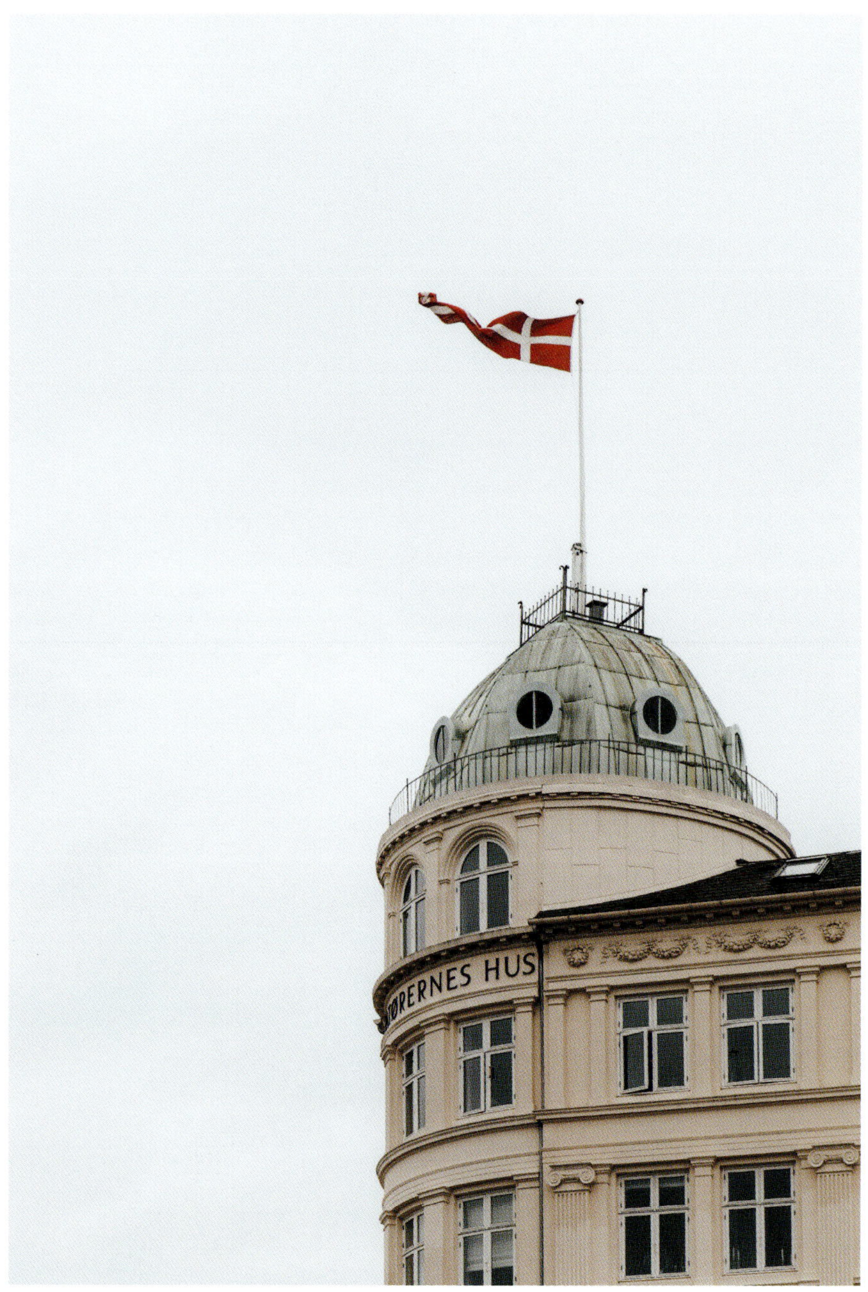

Strolling in the city

Sunday 11:12 AM

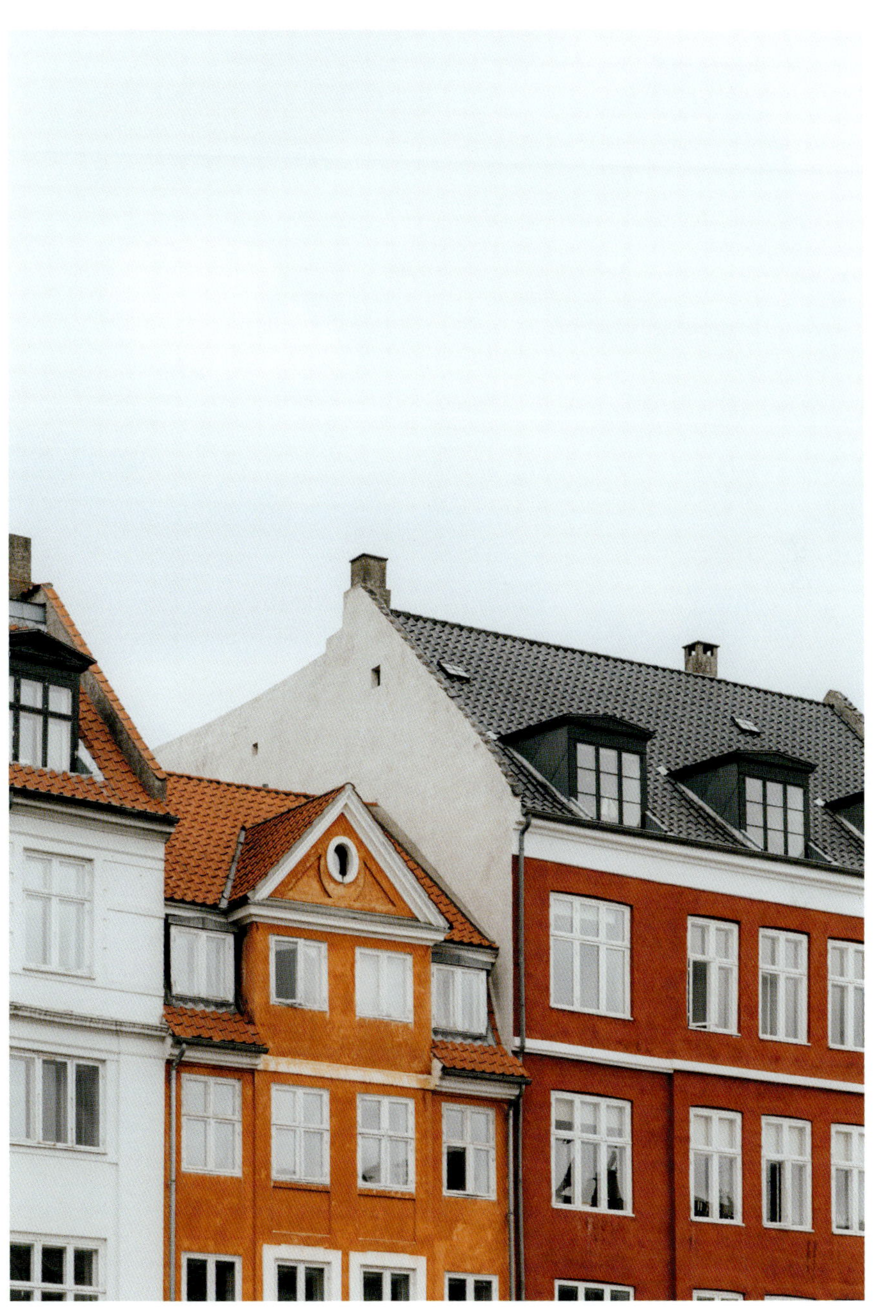

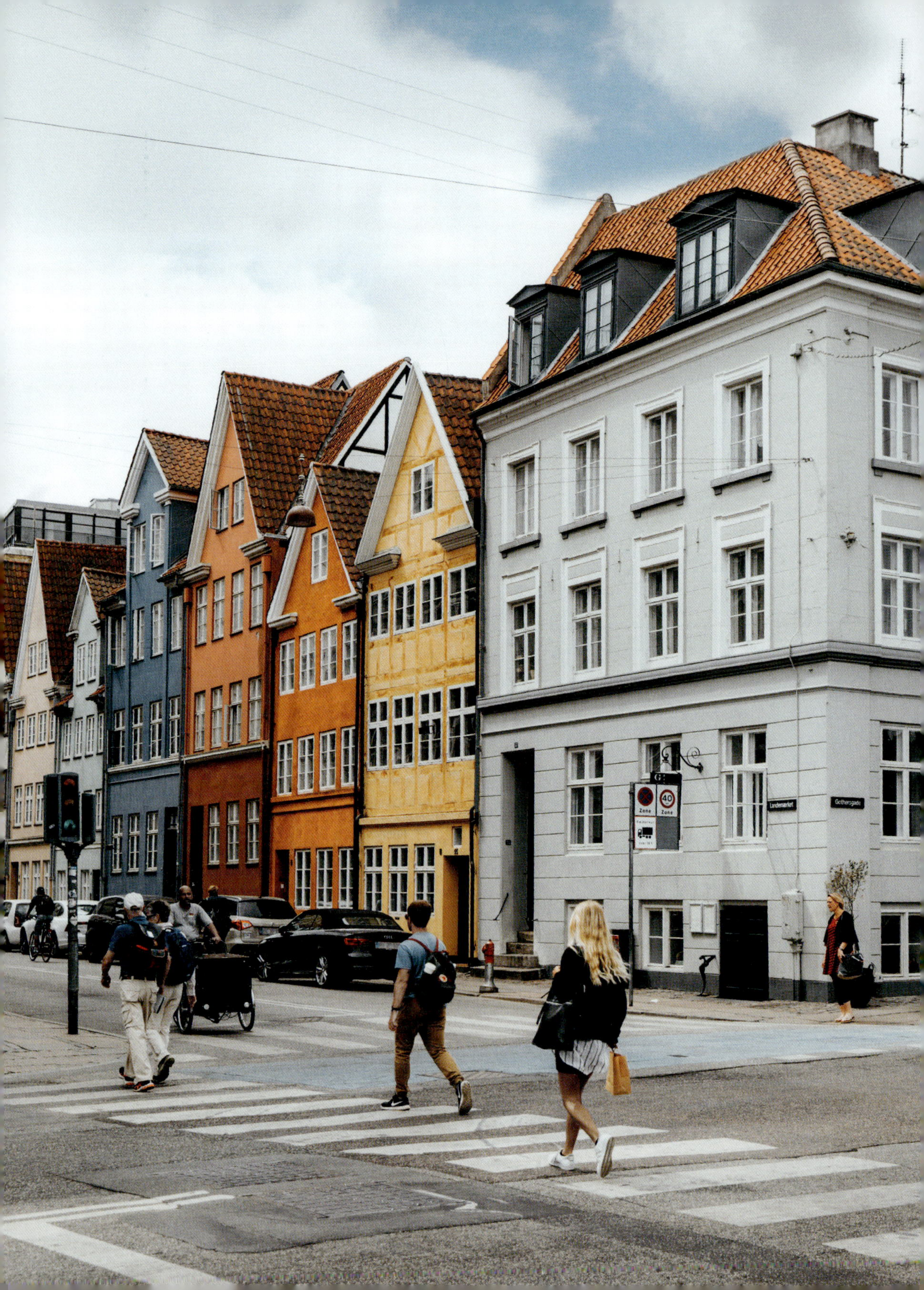
Zone
40
Zone
Gothersgade

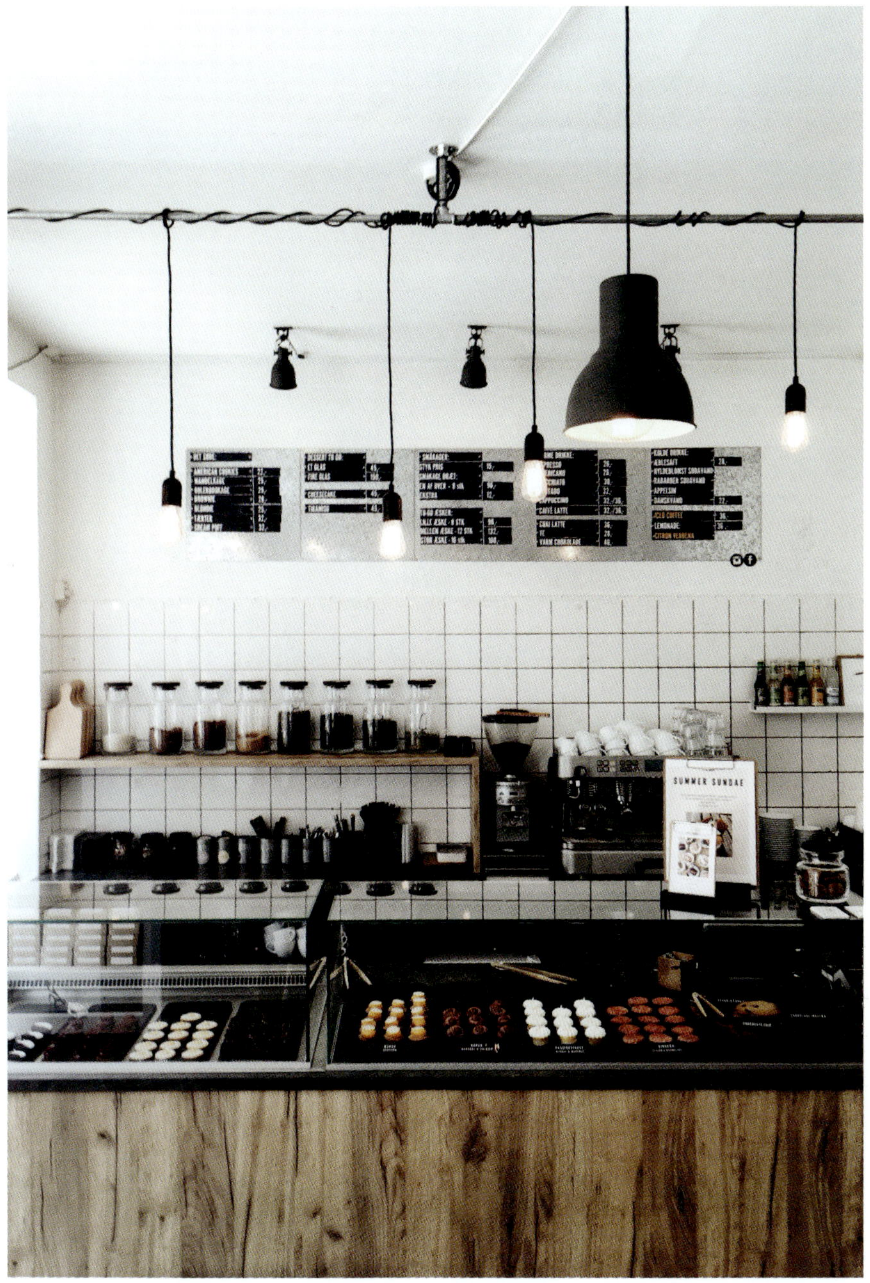

Sunday 11:38 AM

Late morning Danish butter cookie at Leckerbaer

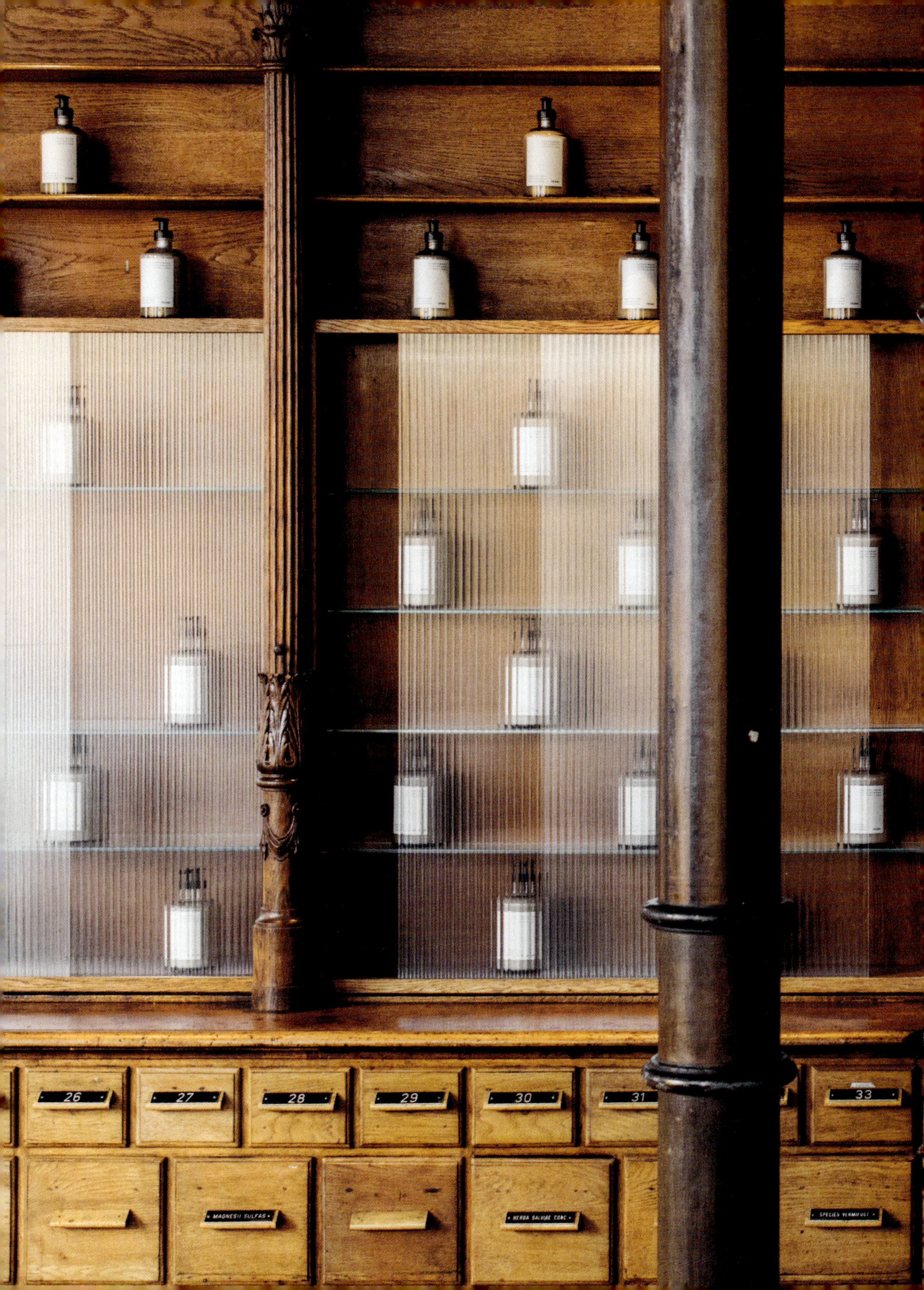
26
27
28
29
30
31
33
MAGNESII SULFAS
HERBA SALVIAE CONC.
SPECIES VERMIFUGI

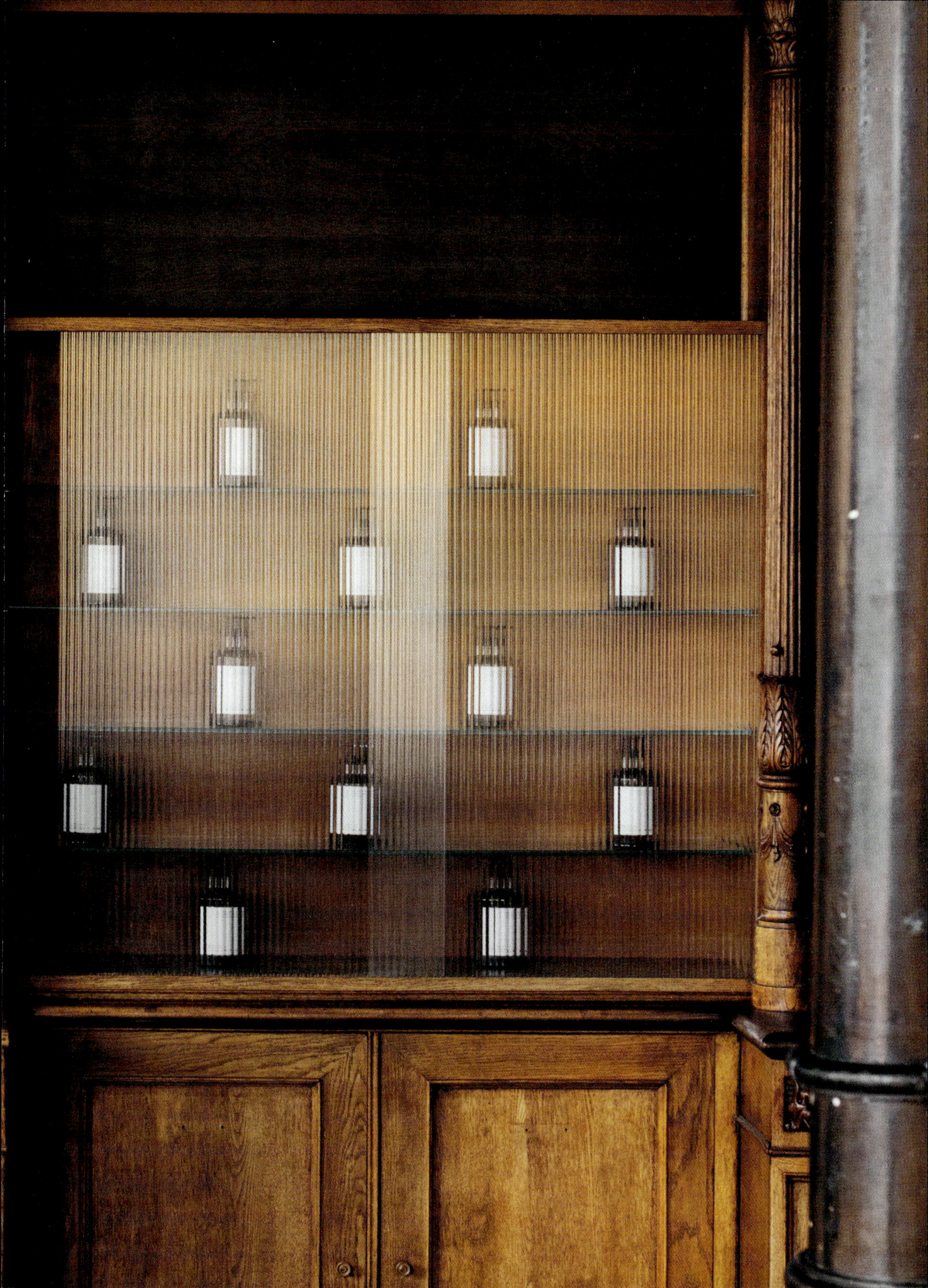

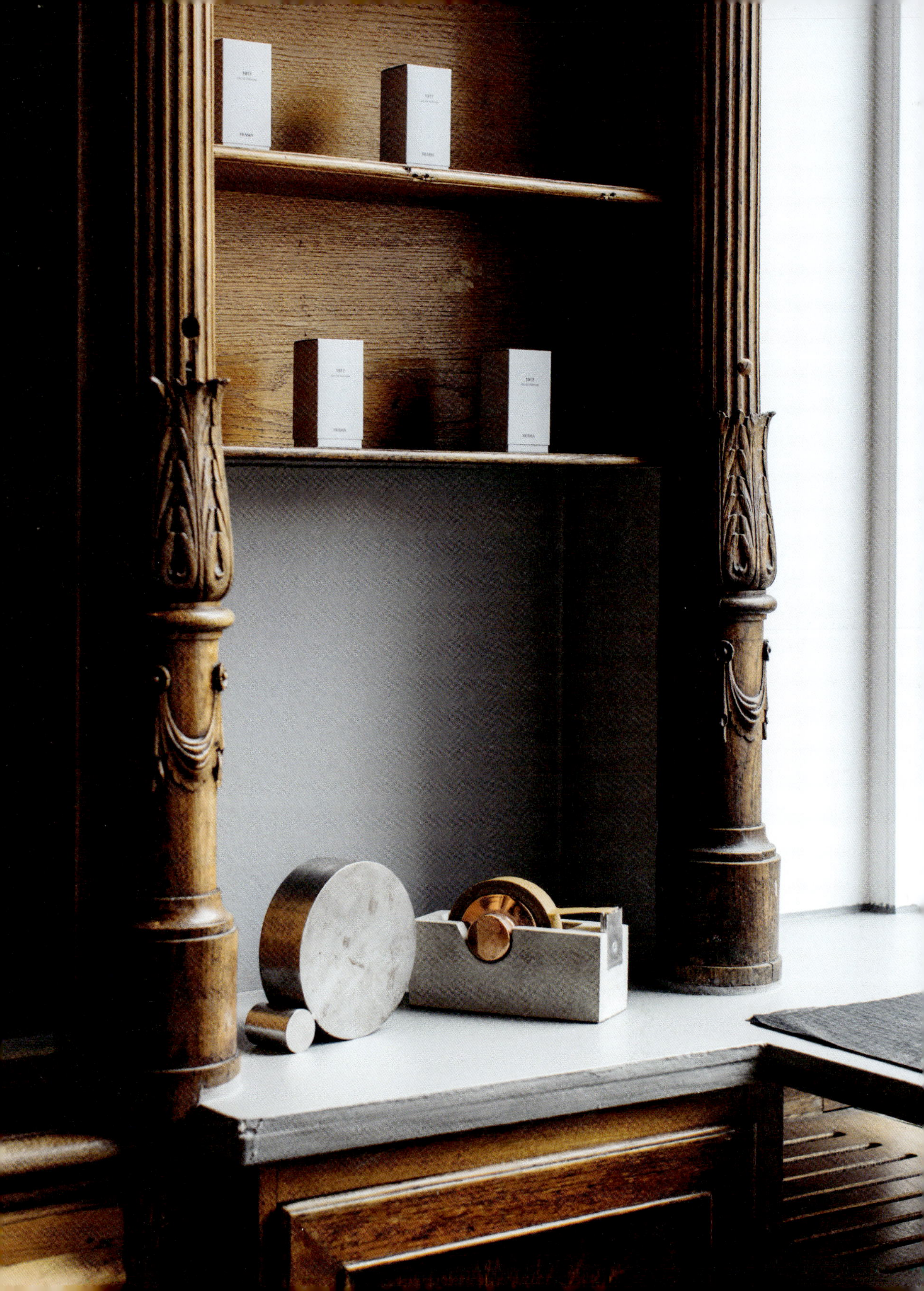

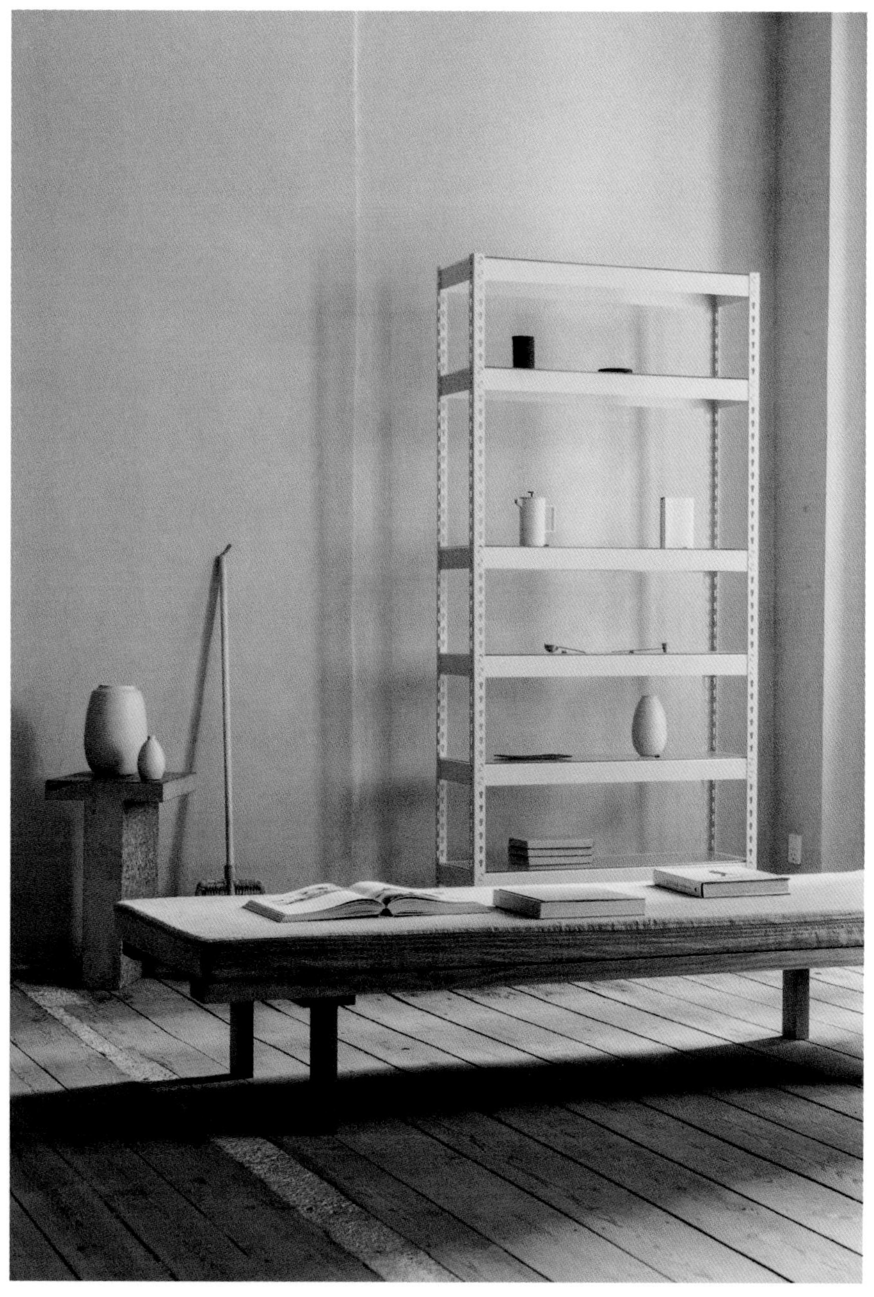

Sunday 12:14 PM

Frama Studio Store

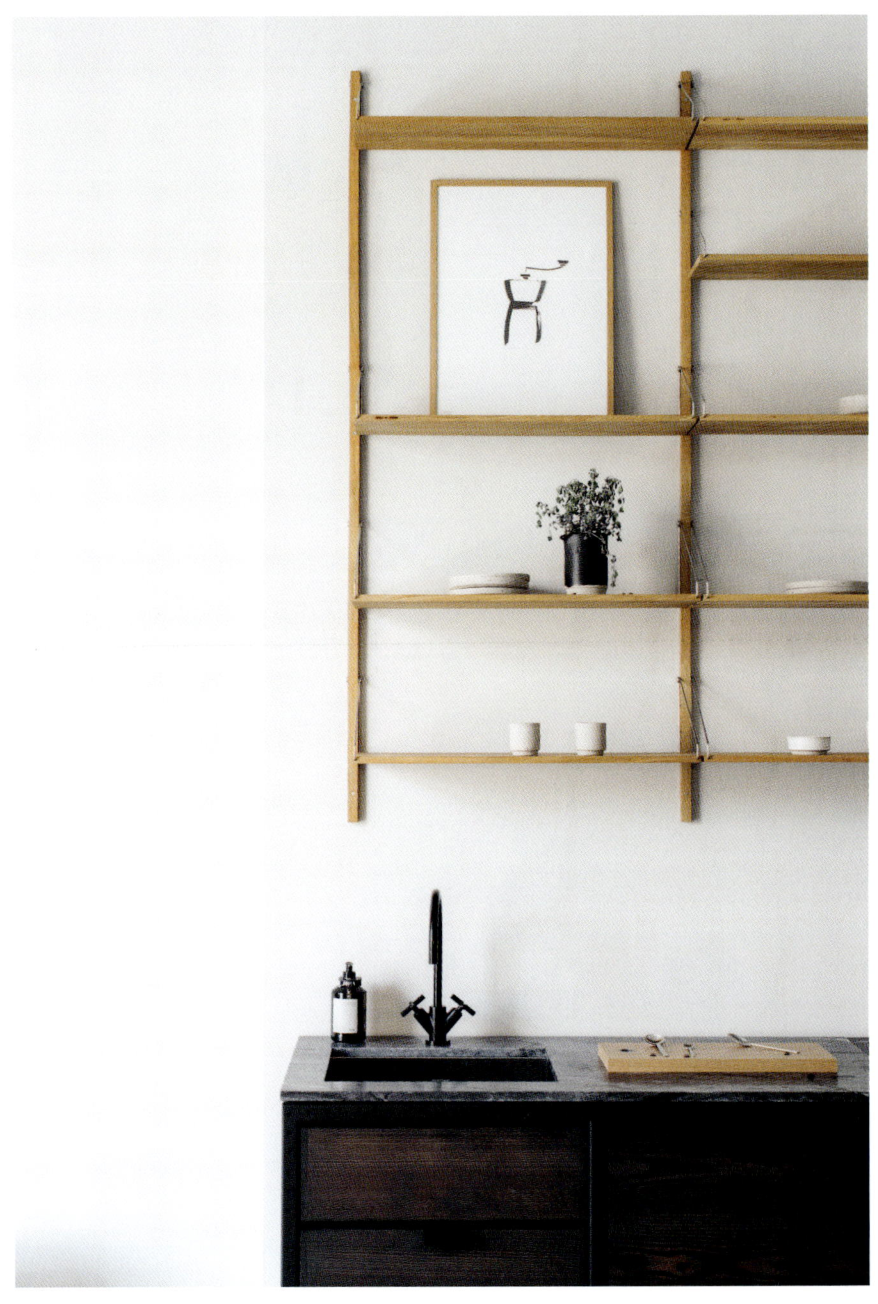

SANDALWOOD
CEDARWOOD
YLANGYLANG
SANDALWOOD
CEDARWOOD
YLANGYLANG
SANDALWOOD
CEDARWOOD
YLANGYLANG
SANDALWOOD
CEDARWOOD
YLANGYLANG

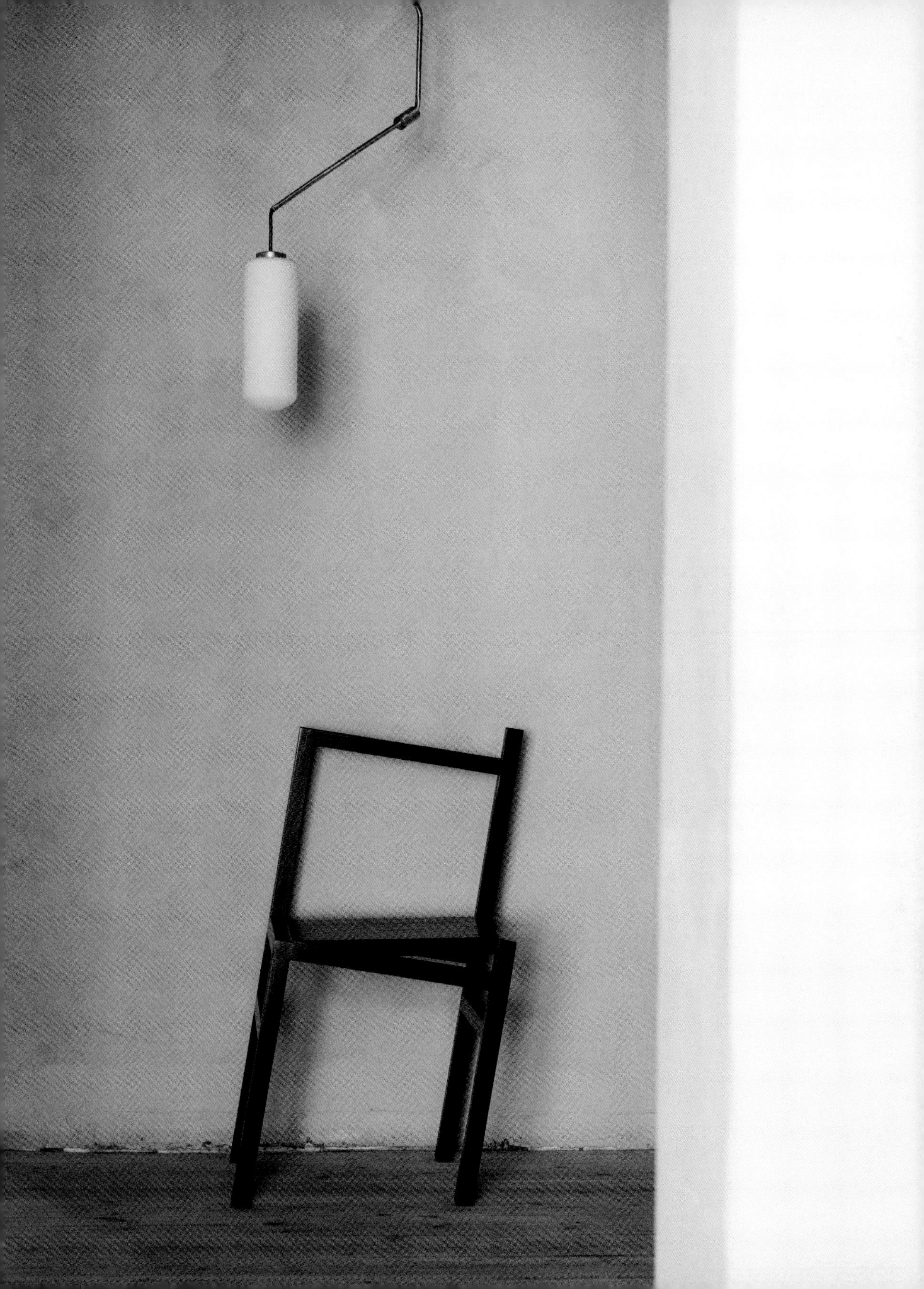

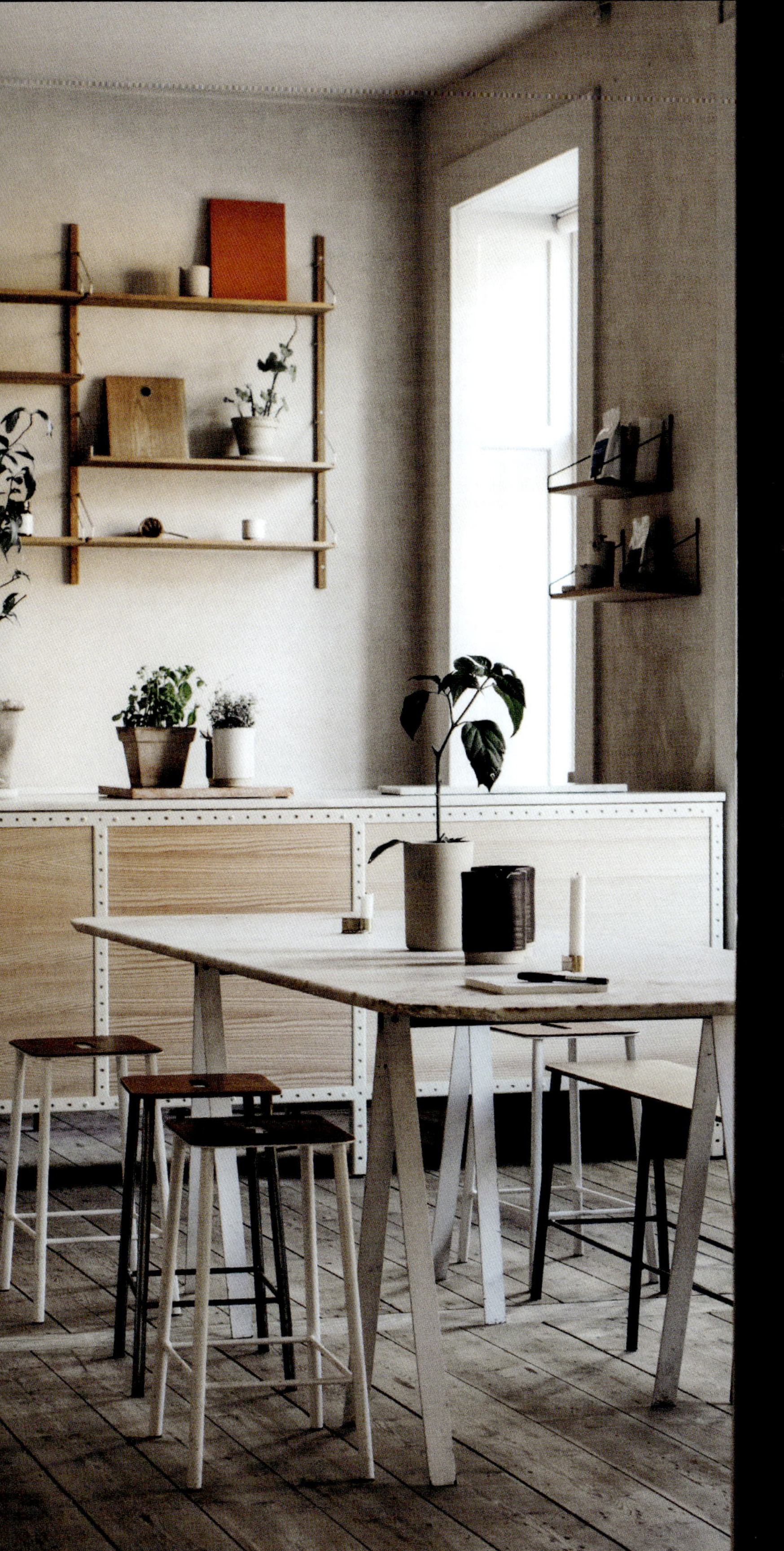

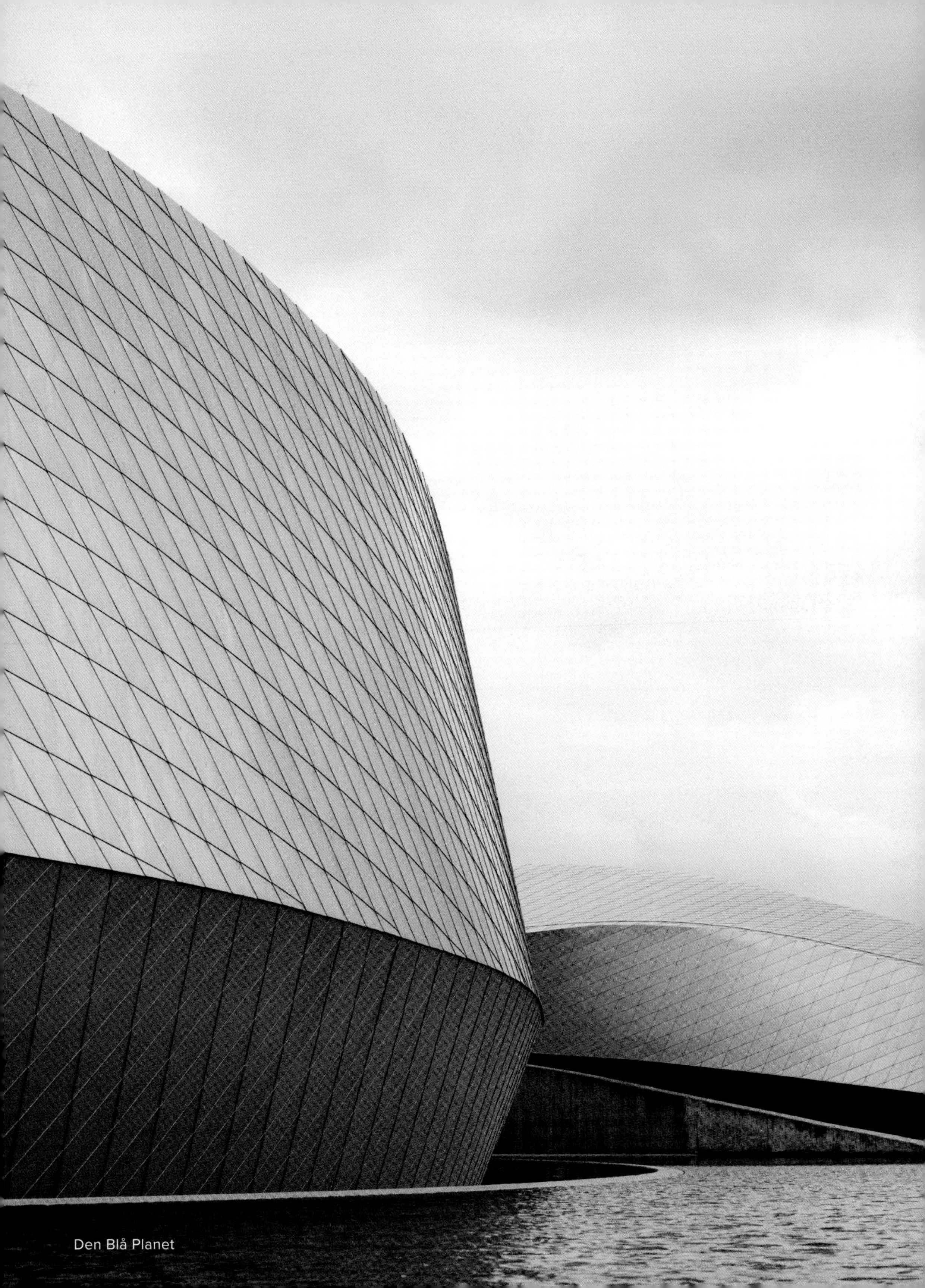

Den Blå Planet

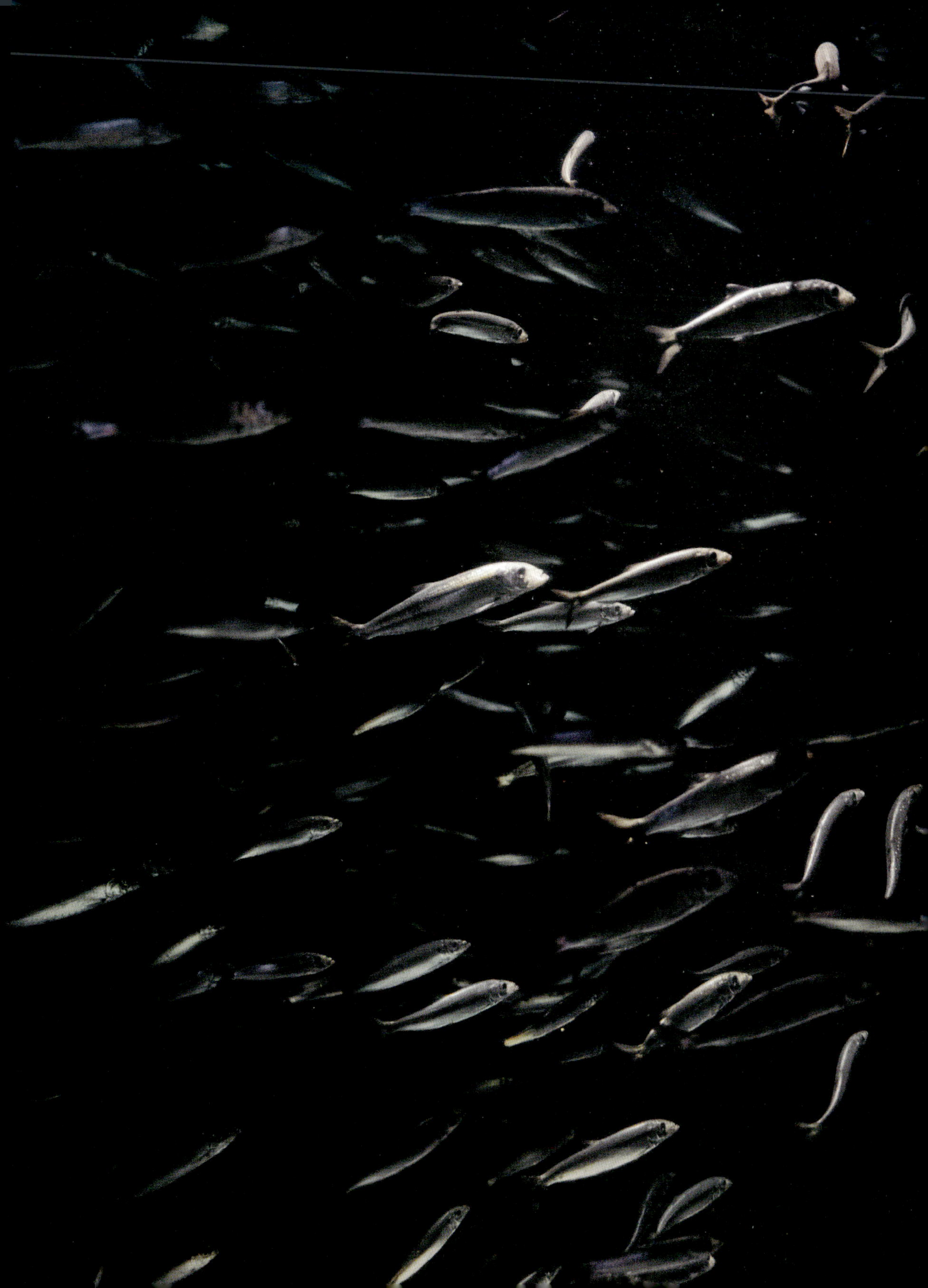

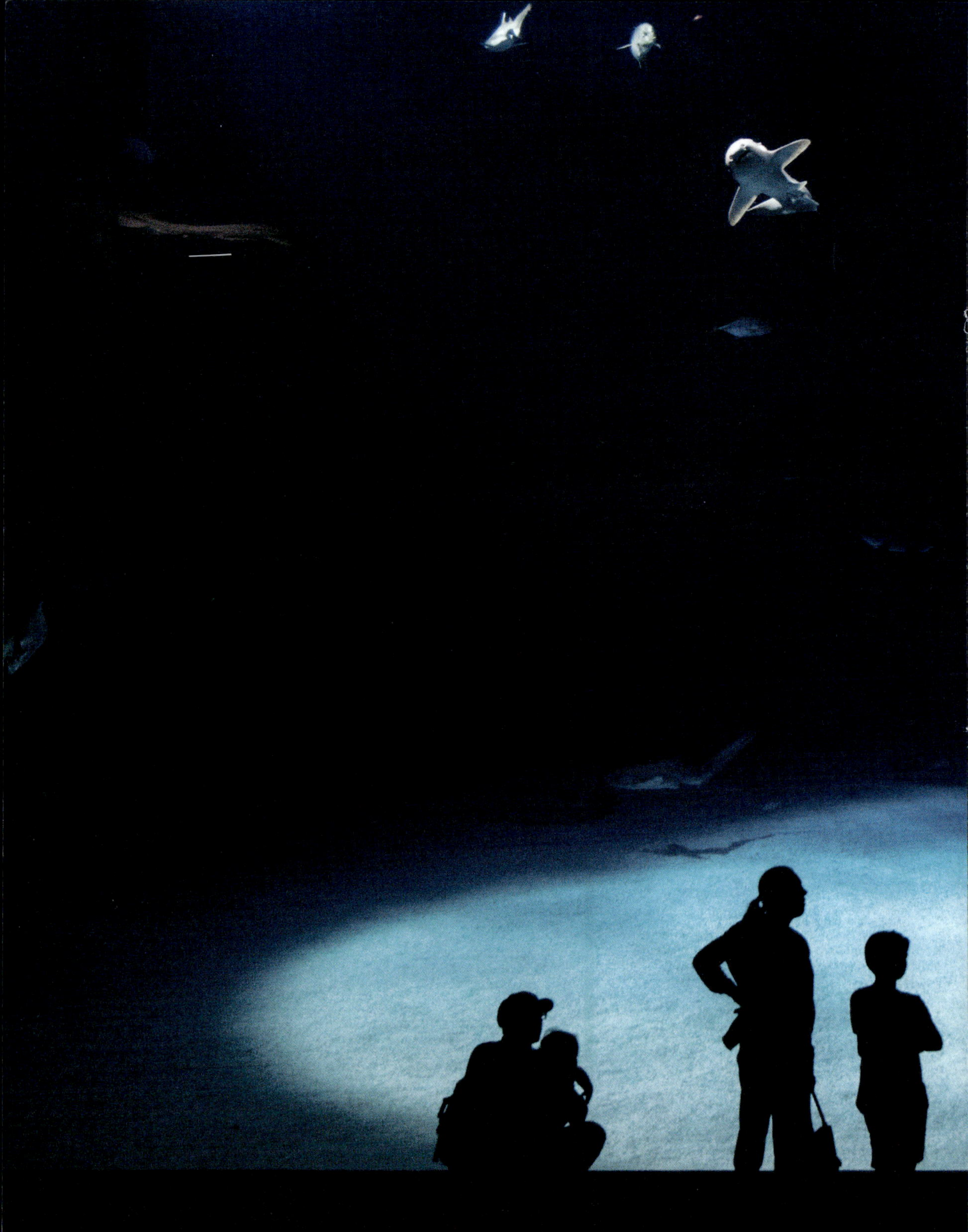

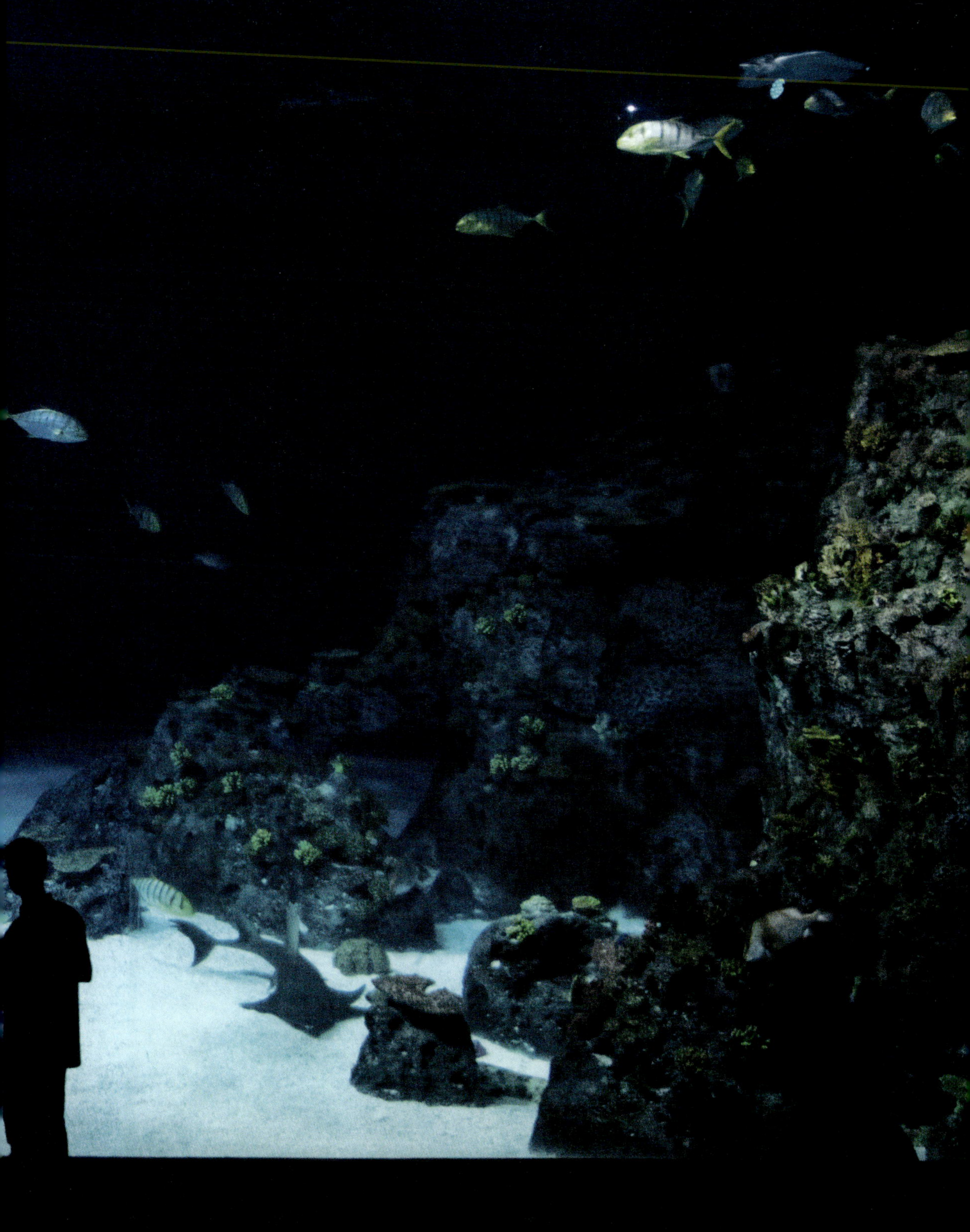

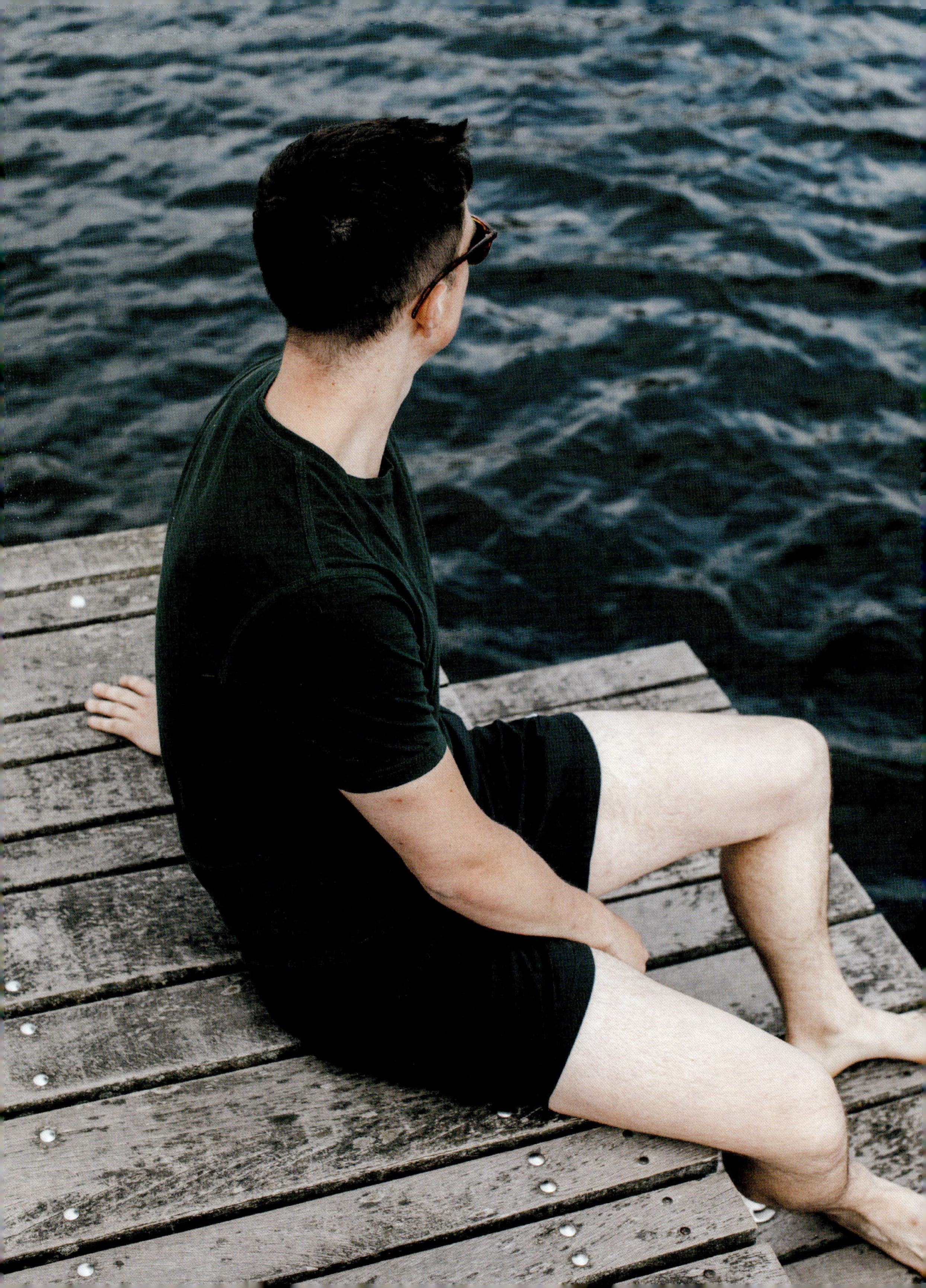

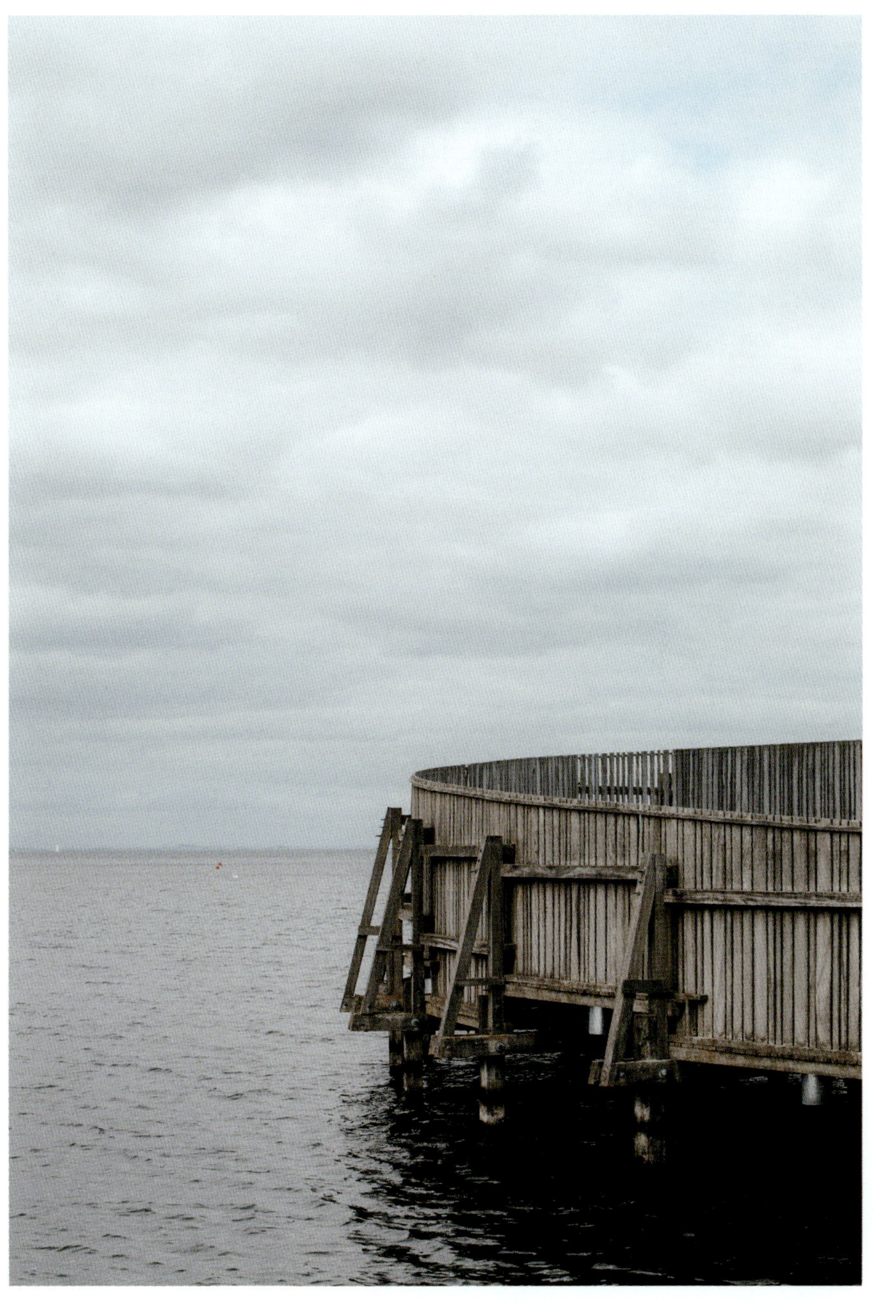

Sunday 3:30 PM

Taking a dip – Kastrup Sea Bath

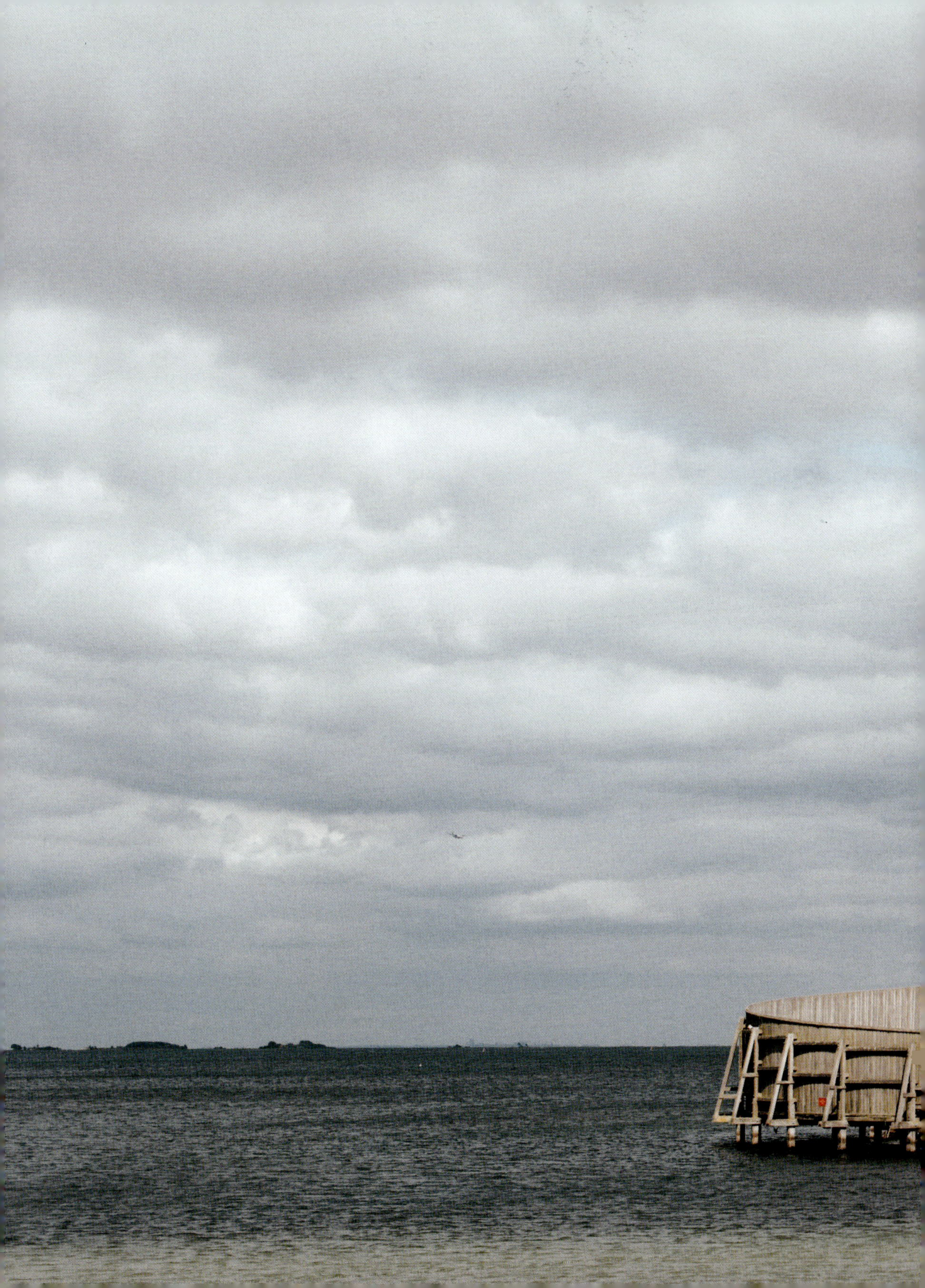

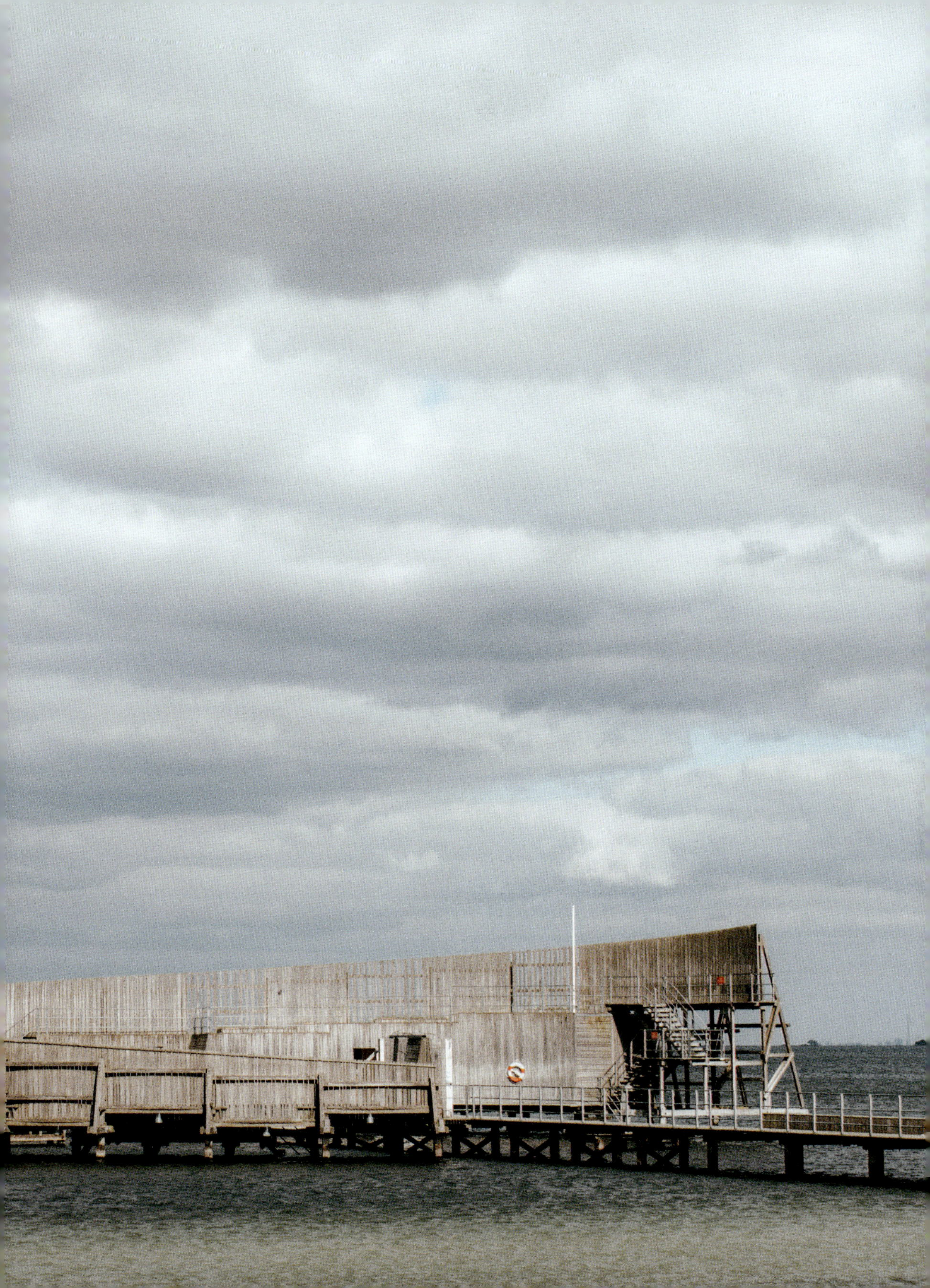

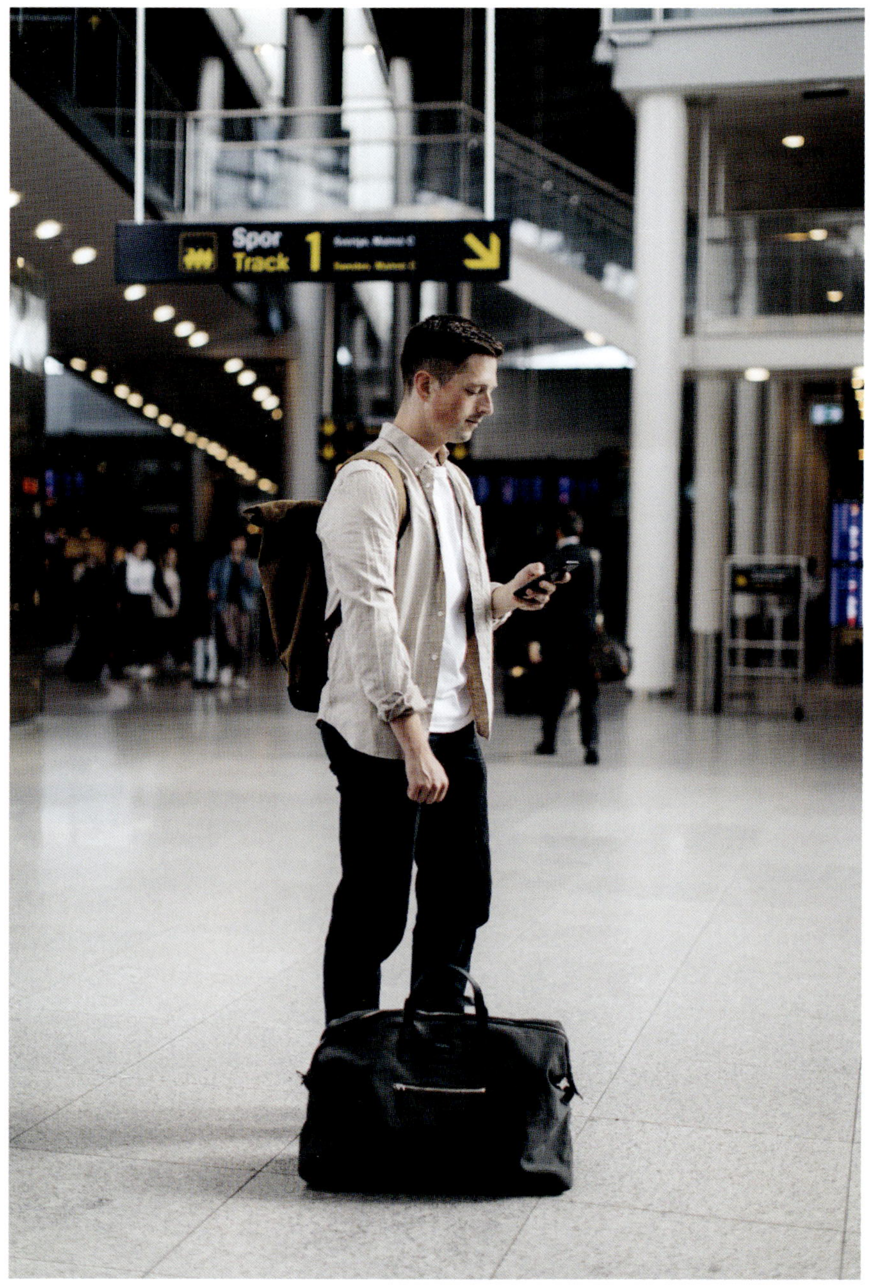

And home

Sunday 6:45 PM

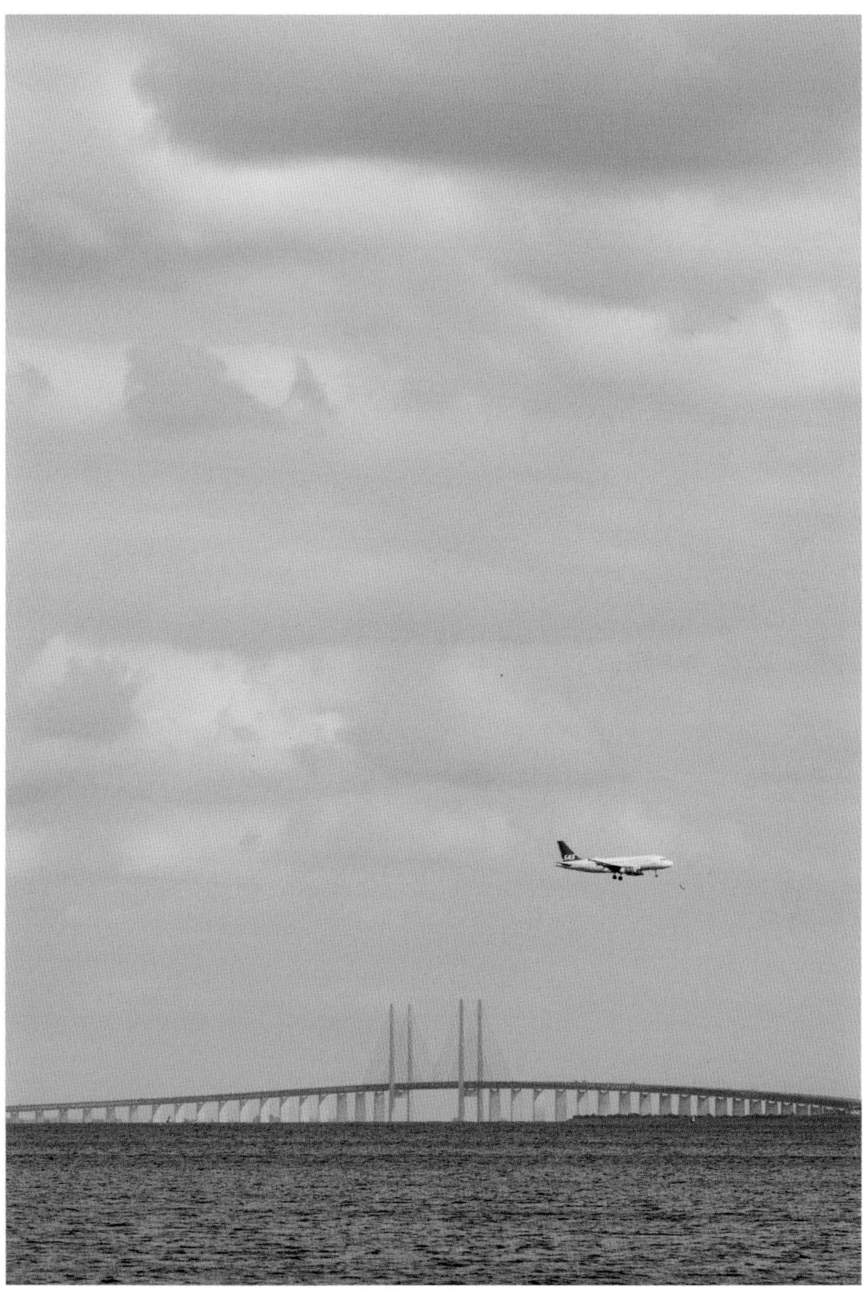

The Weekender

Copenhagen

Published by Lebled Soloviev Editions
(part of New Heroes & Pioneers Publishing)

Photography and text: Toby Mitchell
Creative Direction: Francois Lebled
Book Design: Daniel Zachrisson
Copy Editing: Matt Porter
Model: Matt Porter

Print and bound by BALTO print (Lithuania)
ISBN 9789198941135

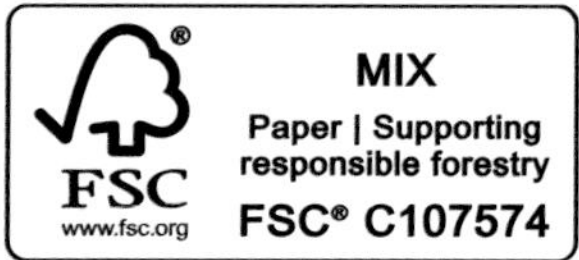

With thanks to:
Francois Le Bled, Matt Porter, Daniel Zachrisson, Jan Kopacz

Sandqvist - sandqvist.com
Hotel Sanders - hotelsanders.com
Frama - framacph.com
Design Museum Denmark - designmuseum.dk
The Kinfolk Gallery - kinfolk.com/gallery
Gasoline Grill - gasolinegrill.com
BÆST - baest.dk

HAY - hay.dk
Østerberg Ice Cream - osterberg-ice.dk
Den Blå Planet - denblaaplanet.dk
WeCycle - wecycle.dk
Vækst - cofoco.dk/en/restaurants/vaekst
Coffee Collective - coffeecollective.dk

COLLECTIVE SHORTS
by NHP PUBLISHING